O COME, ALL YE FAITHFUL

Great Hymns of Our Faith

BOOK 1:

O Worship the King

BOOK 2:

O Come, All Ye Faithful

Hymns of Adoration and Joy to Celebrate His Birth

O Come, All Ye Faithful

JOHN MACARTHUR

JONI EARECKSON TADA

ROBERT & BOBBIE WOLGEMUTH

CROSSWAY BOOKS • WHEATON, ILLINOIS

A DIVISION OF GOOD NEWS PUBLISHERS

LIBRARY OF CONGRESS CATALOGING-IN-PUBLICATION DATA
O come, all ye faithful : hymns of adoration and joy to celebrate His
birth / [compiled by] John MacArthur ... [et al.].
    p.   cm. — (Great hymns of our faith ; bk. 2)
  ISBN 1-58134-251-9
  1. Carols—History and criticism. I. MacArthur, John, 1939-   .
BV530 .02 2001
264'.23—dc21   2001002358
                                                 CIP

15	14	13	12	11	10	09	08	07	06	05	04	03	02	01
15	14	13	12	11	10	9	8	7	6	5	4	3	2	

With gratitude for the musicians who wrote the
time-honored, undying, beautiful tunes that
convey the message of the Christmas
story in these glorious hymns.

JOHN MACARTHUR

———

To Francie Lorey
For all the times you've made the miles go quicker
As we've memorized countless hymns on all our trips.
Thank you for keepin' melody with my harmony.

JONI EARECKSON TADA

———

To our precious girls, Missy and Julie,
with happy memories of caroling—around the tree,
on car trips, visiting nursing homes, and in the neighborhood.
And to their husbands, now our sons, Jon Schrader and
Christopher Tassy, whose strong voices add to the
harmony around the Christmas table.

ROBERT & BOBBIE WOLGEMUTH

———

Special Thanks to:

Mr. John Duncan
of TVP Studios, Greenville, SC,
Executive Producer of the musical recording
for *O Come, All Ye Faithful.*

Dr. Paul Plew
Chairman of the Department of Music
at The Master's College,
who directed the musical production.

The students of The Master's Chorale
who contributed their superb singing skills
and love for these hymns to the CD.

We are deeply grateful for the gifts of these friends
and accomplished professionals.

The publisher's share of income from the *O Come, All Ye Faithful* compact disc is being donated by Good News Publishers/Crossway Books to JAF Ministries, the worldwide disability outreach of Joni Eareckson Tada. For more information about JAF Ministries, please write to JAF Ministries, Post Office Box 3333, Agoura Hills, California 91301 or call 818-707-5664 or go to website—www.joniandfriends.org

---

TABLE OF CONTENTS

FOREWORD

Quite an unusual story lies behind the writing of the books in this series. But then we might expect as much because the authors—Joni Eareckson Tada, John MacArthur, and Robert and Bobbie Wolgemuth—are such extraordinary people!

In the broadest sense this book is the story of God's unfailing faithfulness, as told in the great hymns of the faith and in the stories that lie behind these hymns. Whether written in the midst of overwhelming tragedy or in moments of great joy, the hymns in the books in this series have profoundly touched the lives of Christians through the centuries—and they will do so again as these books are read.

But the immediate story behind this series starts (as many unusual stories do!) with our very dear friend Joni Eareckson Tada. Joni, as you know, broke her neck in a diving accident when she was seventeen years old, and she has lived as a quadriplegic for more than three decades ever since. But by God's grace and through Joni's perseverance, she lives a most extraordinary life—a life that above all else reflects the joy of the Lord. One of my favorite memories, in fact, is stopping with Joni in hotel lobbies to sing impromptu hymns of praise and worship— to the delight and sometimes wonder of other hotel guests.

The occasion that gave birth to this series of books and accompanying CDs, then, was *Joni's* idea—this time to sing "impromptu hymns" with Dr. John MacArthur at the Good News-Crossway 60th Anniversary Banquet, in the summer of 1998. The theme for the banquet was "Celebrating Sixty Years of God's Faithfulness," and both Joni and John MacArthur, Joni's pastor and close friend, were scheduled to speak. Joni and John checked with me first to be sure it was okay—and of course Joni doesn't take "no" for an answer! But it came as a complete surprise to everyone else when Joni invited John to join her on the platform to sing an "impromptu" duet of their favorite hymns.

Rarely have I seen an audience so deeply moved. As they listened to Joni sing the praises of God's faithfulness, it was a remarkable moment—a moment when we were all given a glimpse of God's glory.

Immediately after the banquet I started urging John and Joni to make a CD of hymns. And from there the ideas just kept growing. Joni invited her friends Robert and Bobbie Wolgemuth to join in since, as Joni noted, "We've sung together for years . . . over the telephone, in hotel lobbies, in restaurant parking lots, and they'd love to be part of this." And of course we'd need a book to go with the CD. But there are so many great hymns, we soon realized we'd really need *four* books!

All these ideas have come together in a most exciting way for each book so far. The recording studio was booked; John MacArthur brought Dr. Paul Plew and the highly acclaimed Chorale of Master's College; and Joni, John, Robert, and Bobbie joined in singing some of the greatest hymns of all time. As Joni reflected after recording the CD for the first book, *O Worship the King*, "The adventure of singing together was pure delight. It was two solid days of worship and praise."

Now, several years after Joni "cooked up" her idea for a duet, her idea continues to come to life in the books in this series and in the CDs tucked into the back covers. It is our prayer that through these books and CDs you will also see a glimpse of God's glory and discover a deeper understanding of His faithfulness, and that you would join with Joni and John and Robert and Bobbie—and indeed the Church of our Lord Jesus Christ through the centuries—in singing the praises of our Lord and Savior.

O come, all ye faithful, joyful and triumphant . . .
O come, let us adore him, Christ the Lord.

Lane T. Dennis, Ph.D.
Publisher

INTRODUCTION

You've probably never heard of Bernie Felstead. But the firsthand account of his experience near the village of Laventie in Northern France captivates all who read it. It's a story Bernie recalled to a reporter as crisply as if it had happened last year. Even at 102, the only living eyewitness, his eyes sparkled at the retelling of an event that had taken place more than eight decades before.

It was a bitter cold morning, December 25, 1914. A twenty-one-year-old private in the Royal Welsh infantry, Bernie was holding his ground in a trench, along with hundreds of brothers-in-arms—young men longing to be home at Christmas. Hostile German troops were barely a hundred yards away.

The evening before—Christmas Eve—the gunfire had begun to subside. Just before dawn, silence suspended itself like a great mist over the battleground. A lone German soldier began singing the Welsh song, "All Through the Night." His silken tenor voice pierced the darkness as he sang the words in English.

> *Sleep, my child, and peace attend thee*
> *All through the night.*
> *Guardian angels God will send thee*
> *All through the night.*
> *Soft the drowsy hours are creeping,*
> *Hill and vale in slumber sleeping,*
> *God his loving vigil keeping*
> *All through the night.*

Bernie Felstead and his comrades listened in amazement. Five months of relentless gunfire had, for the moment, been replaced with a Christmas carol their mothers had tenderly sung to them as little boys. Deep emotion filled their hearts.

Presently one of Felstead's fellow soldiers a few yards away began singing another Christmas carol, his hearty reply in flawless German.

"The Germans came out of their trenches and walked over to us," Bernie remembered. "Nobody decided for us. We just climbed over our parapets and went over to them. We weren't afraid."

Bernie remembered how foreboding the Germans looked with their strange spiked helmets. Very few British troops knew any German, and hardly a German spoke a single word in English. "But," said Bernie, his leathered face now hinting at the emotion that must have filled his heart that morning, "without any spoken orders we all agreed we would not fight that day."

The soldiers exchanged greetings and shook hands, wishing each other a happy Christmas. For a few hours, armies of angels seemed to hover over the battlefield. "Peace on earth" had her way. And Bernie Felstead lived to tell the story.

Exactly thirty years later at the battlefront near Elsenborn Ridge, Belgium, Lt. Charles Stockell, a forward artillery observer for the 2nd Division, was holed up at company headquarters. At 11:45 on Christmas Eve, the gunfire slowly died down. "At the stroke of midnight," Charles later recalled, "without an order or a request . . . voices were raised in the old familiar Christmas carols."

Almost as though on cue from the Savior Himself, heavy snowflakes fell softly, blanketing the weapons. The white cover gave the signs of war a festive brilliance in the moonlight.

The infantry held their front-line positions. Soon they could hear voices less than 200 yards away in the darkness. German soldiers lifted their voices clear and strong. And as they sang, the troops from both sides joined in.

Silent night! Holy night!
All is calm, all is bright
Round yon virgin mother and child.

Holy infant, so tender and mild,
Sleep in heavenly peace,
Sleep in heavenly peace.

For a moment frozen in time, these young men's souls were warmed and comforted by the holy presence of the Christ-child.

You can tell when Christmas is coming. It's a season like no other.

"Hark! the Herald Angels Sing" rings out as the wheels on your grocery cart flop in time down the polished aisle. The air at the shopping malls or office buildings is filled with familiar holiday tunes. Memories of Grandma's apple pie and family gathered 'round the table fill us with anticipation. "Angels We Have Heard on High" descends from ceiling speakers at the pharmacy counter or in Housewares and Small Appliances at our favorite department store. The words to the carol roll through our memories. It makes us happy.

This music changes everything.

For some the memory of these hymns at Christmas really *did* stop the fighting. The tender birth of the Savior and the fathomless power of God's incarnate Son calmed the siege. Like the snow, peace descended on the battlefields.

And this peace that passes understanding still restores our hearts.

The Christmas carols and the stories in this book provide a setting for the truth of the Bible story. Our hope is that they will bring new meaning to the old familiar songs you love.

We join you in the celebration. Peace on earth . . . Jesus Christ is born.

God bless us, everyone!

Joni Eareckson Tada, Agoura Hills, California

John MacArthur, Sun Valley, California

Robert & Bobbie Wolgemuth, Orlando, Florida

O Come, All Ye Faithful

JOHN FRANCIS WADE

1711-1786

O come, all ye faithful, joyful and triumphant,
O come ye, O come ye to Bethlehem;
Come and behold him born the King of angels;
O come, let us adore him, O come, let us adore him,
O come, let us adore him, Christ the Lord.

God of God, Light of Light;
Lo, he abhors not the Virgin's womb;
Very God, begotten, not created;
O come, let us adore him, O come, let us adore him,
O come, let us adore him, Christ the Lord.

Sing, choirs of angels, sing in exultation,
Sing, all ye citizens of heav'n above;
Glory to God in the highest;
O come, let us adore him, O come, let us adore him,
O come, let us adore him, Christ the Lord.

Yea, Lord, we greet thee, born this happy morning:
Jesus, to thee be all glory giv'n;
Word of the Father, late in flesh appearing;
O come, let us adore him, O come, let us adore him,
O come, let us adore him, Christ the Lord.

At the Heart of the Hymn

Robert Wolgemuth

.ℓ

*That which was from the beginning, which we have heard, which we have
seen with our eyes, which we have looked at and our hands have touched—this
we proclaim concerning the Word of life.*

—1 John 1:1

*I*F YOU'VE TRAVELED DURING THE DAYS that lead up to Christmas, you
know that it's the busiest time of the year for every kind of transportation imag-
inable. From horse-carts to jumbo jets, this is the season when people do whatever they can to be together.

Over the past few decades, as technology has advanced, some speculated that
Christmas travel would slow down. Cellular telephones, fax machines, and dig-
ital images of family members screaming over the Internet might give people a
reason *not* to go to the trouble of packing suitcases and making long trips. Virtual
reunions just might do the trick and replace the real thing. Not a chance.

We don't need the National Transportation and Safety Board in Washington
to tell us what we already know if we've traveled at Christmas. Electronically
transmitted voices, messages, and images just aren't the same. We long to actually *be* together . . . to literally see and hold each other. So we'll do what's necessary to make the trip. And we can hardly wait.

And speaking of waiting, one of the great adventures of childbirth is the
anticipation of our first encounter with our baby. As a daddy and a granddaddy,
I've been through this experience several times. I have watched my wife's and
my daughters' tummies swell as their babies grew and developed. And I have been

filled with the same kind of eager anticipation I feel at the end of the long trip home. "Joyful" and "triumphant" describe this feeling very well.

I'll never forget a conversation I had during the final weeks of our daughter's last pregnancy. Missy said to me, "I just can't wait to see his face. I can't wait to hold him."

One of the things I love about Christmas is that travel and childbirth are inextricably linked to each other. The purpose of all the travel—by shepherds and wise men—was to visit a baby. The Christ-child was born. And the consummate focus of Mary's and Joseph's anticipation was to see His precious face and to feel the weight of His tiny body in their waiting arms.

What I love about this carol is that it speaks of our coming to the Savior—of travel and of deep contemplation. Time on the road and time on our knees. "O come, let us adore him."

During the month of December, our home church is busy with all sorts of opportunities for worship. Special services, concerts, and pageants fill the calendar. Together with our family and our friends, we gather to sing and praise the Savior's birth.

But in the quietness of our own hearts, with the same intimacy of an expectant mother longing to see her baby's face, we adore the Redeemer who, by His grace, has literally taken up residence in our hearts.

"O come, let us adore him."

Like a great magnet, Christmas draws us together. The sounds and the smells of busy households preparing for great feasts are such a familiar part of this happy season. Nothing will ever replace this joy.

But Christmas also draws us to worship and revere Him . . . to see *His* face and to know and love Him.

IN THE LIGHT OF THE WORD

John MacArthur

◦⌒

THIS FAMILIAR AND WELL-LOVED HYMN is a summons to worship the incarnate God. It reminds us that the baby who was born in Bethlehem was "the King of angels"—none other than God in the flesh.

The titles given Him in the second stanza are potent: "God of God," "Light of Light," and "very God, begotten, not created." Those are all deliberate echoes of the Nicene Creed, which speaks of Christ in these terms:

> *God from God, Light from Light,*
> *true God from true God,*
> *begotten, not made,*
> *of one Being with the Father.*
> *Through him all things were made.*

The begetting spoken of by both the hymn and the Creed is not the begetting of the human Christ in the womb of Mary. Nor does it refer to any kind of pro-creation or act of generation that took place in time. Rather, it speaks of an eternal relationship between Father and Son. It is the same thing Scripture describes when it calls Christ "the only begotten of the Father" (John 1:14). It is the very basis for Christ's repeated claims of absolute equality with the Father (cf. John 8:58; 10:30; 14:9).

The final stanza employs yet another title that signifies Christ's deity: "Word of the Father." That is a reference to the opening verses of John's Gospel: "In the beginning was the Word, and the Word was with God, and the Word was God. He was in the beginning with God. . . . And the Word became flesh and dwelt among us, and we beheld His glory, the glory as of the only begotten of the Father, full of grace and truth" (1:1-2, 14).

Why did John call Jesus "the Word"? Because it would meet all His hearers on a common ground. "Word" would speak to the Jews because they knew the Word of God was that by which God created the universe. To them the Word was the power, the will, and the mind of God directed to fulfilling His purposes.

So John is saying to his Jewish readers, "If you want to see the Word of God that creates, the Word that spoke the universe into existence, the Word that reveals the mind of God to men, the Word that gives life and light to the soul, look at Jesus Christ. He *is* that Word! In Him, Jesus Christ, the Word of God came to you!"

"Word" would also speak to the Greeks. According to Greek philosophy the divine *logos* (Word) was the manifest power of deity, the instrument through which the world was made. Although the Greeks thought of the *logos* as an impersonal force, they nonetheless believed the Word was the very embodiment of divine power—that which created and sustains the entire cosmos.

So John pointed to Christ as the personification of the divine Word. This corrected the Greeks' notion of the *logos* as an impersonal force, and it corrected the Jews' expectation of a merely human Messiah.

For centuries both Jews and Greeks had been thinking, writing, and contemplating the *logos*—the power of the universe, the sum and source of all real wisdom, sound reason, and absolute truth. Jesus Christ is that Word, come to earth as a man! By using "Word" to identify Jesus, John is stating plainly who He really is: the very mind and power of God. He is God revealed to humanity.

The hymn-writer picks up this reference in His call to worship, because it is the ultimate biblical expression of Christ's deity, which is the theme of the hymn. "The Word was God" (John 1:1).

So the hymn masterfully blends the worship of the angels ("Glory to God in the highest," Luke 2:13) with the worship of the shepherds ("Yea, Lord, we greet thee"). All of it emphasizes that Christ is the Lord, the One worthy of all our adoration.

"O come, let us adore him, Christ the Lord."

FROM OUT OF THE PAST
Bobbie Wolgemuth

THERE HAS BEEN SOME MYSTERY behind the writing of this favorite carol calling the faithful to come. It was written by an English layman who was known for his elegant, hand-drawn calligraphy and manuscript copying. John Francis Wade would take Latin meditations and Scripture and weave them together with Anglican chants and Gregorian tones to write Catholic masses.

The original text, *"Adestes Fideles,"* was in Latin and was set to a distinctive musical form of the medieval church called "plainchant." Wade was a scholar of plainchant and produced so many liturgical books and manuscripts for the Catholic Church that he became known as the father of plainchant revival.

Historians have found several interesting masses with Wade's signature; one has been labeled the "Jacobite manuscript." In his early thirties, Wade and others were sympathetic to the Jacobite cause in England. He wrote masses to promote the return of exiled sympathizers. Wade and the Jacobites longed for military success against those who held the British throne.

Historians believe that Wade could have secretly slipped into these masses the words calling on the faithful to come together for political enforcement. Printed in the margins of "O Come, All Ye Faithful," he called faithful Jacobites to arms in a rallying cry on the eve of the rebellion of 1745.

The rich, full, rolling tones with which we sing this carol today are probably from a popular Portuguese hymn tune. The Latin text, meaning to "be present or near, you faithful," was so appealing to Frederick Oakeley, an Anglican minister, that he translated it into English for his own congregation. It was 100 years after Wade wrote the words that Oakeley gave his church, and English-speaking people, the translation we now enjoy. With its full military sound, it has become a favorite processional carol for Christmas Eve services.

Now translated into languages worldwide, it is still a rallying cry for the faithful to come with allegiance and worship the true King. "O come, let us adore him."

Once in Royal David's City

CECIL FRANCES ALEXANDER
1818-1895

Once in royal David's city stood a lowly cattle shed,
Where a mother laid her baby in a manger for his bed:
Mary was that mother mild, Jesus Christ her little child.

He came down to earth from heaven who is God and Lord of all,
And his shelter was a stable, and his cradle was a stall:
With the poor, and mean, and lowly, lived on earth our Savior holy.

And through all his wondrous childhood he would honor and obey,
Love and watch the lowly maiden in whose gentle arms he lay:
Christian children all must be mild, obedient, good as he.

And our eyes at last shall see him, through his own redeeming love;
For that child so dear and gentle is our Lord in heav'n above,
And he leads his children on to the place where he is gone.

Not in that poor lowly stable, with the oxen standing by,
We shall see him, but in heaven, set at God's right hand on high;
When like stars his children crowned all in white shall wait around.

AT THE HEART OF THE HYMN
Joni Eareckson Tada

℘

The LORD is my shepherd, I shall lack nothing.

He makes me lie down in green pastures,

he leads me beside quiet waters, he restores my soul.

He guides me in paths of righteousness for his name's sake.

—PSALM 23:1-3

TWO MOONLIT FIGURES, one perched atop a donkey, wound their way down a dark road toward the village of Bethlehem. Mary was relieved the long journey was nearly over. Every time her donkey stumbled, she clutched her swollen abdomen.

Who could blame her for being a little frightened? Joseph hadn't said much about where they would stay the night. He halted the donkey and stepped aside to let others pass. Mary pressed both her hands against her back and straightened for a moment to relieve her stiffness. More people streamed by, leading camels and donkeys loaded with supplies. Her eyes met Joseph's—it was obvious the overnight lodges in Bethlehem would be crowded. Joseph gathered the donkey's reins, and they proceeded.

I like to picture that scene. It makes the Holy Family seem so *human*. And had I been a traveler walking behind Mary, perhaps I would have heard the young woman atop the donkey murmur familiar words: "The Lord is my shepherd, I shall not want . . . yea, though I walk through the valley . . . your rod and your staff, they comfort me." Being a fellow citizen of Bethlehem, I would recognize it as the 23rd Psalm.

It's not remarkable to think that Mary would have turned to God's Word on that rough road. She was in pain. What better time to quote a consoling Scripture. And what better Scripture than the 23rd Psalm? Every young Jewish woman (especially one familiar with Bethlehem, the royal city of David) would know that the surrounding hills, speckled with shepherds and their flocks of sheep, served as David's inspiration for the Psalm. Mary, if anyone, would realize that King David had been a resident in Bethlehem a thousand years earlier.

And so picture it. From a distance Mary sees the housetops of Bethlehem washed in moonlight. As she looks up into the hills during that last mile, her heart is warmed to think of David tending his sheep on those same pastures. She glimpses the campfires of the shepherds and is reminded of the Great Shepherd watching over her. Little does she know that, just hours later, the clouds above those same fields will part, heaven will open, and an angel—many angels—will shatter the silence to announce the birth of God's Son.

What encouraged Mary that night? After they arrived at the stable, she was no doubt cold and weary. As Joseph helped her onto a bed of straw, did she gird her heart, repeating, "The Lord is my shepherd. . . . He makes me to lie down . . ."? When she heard the clattering of hooves on stone—Roman soldiers passing by—did she quiet her nerves and pray, "You prepare a table before me in the presence of my enemies. You anoint my head with oil; my cup overflows"?

After Jesus was born and she cradled Him in her arms, did she know she was holding the Lamb of God who would one day take away the sins of the world? The Good Shepherd who would lay down His life for His sheep? I wonder if the visit from the shepherds was God's way of gently reminding her, "Mary, the Lord is *your* Shepherd."

"Once in royal David's city stood a lowly cattle shed, where a mother laid her baby in a manger for his bed." No, I don't believe it's a stretch to think that the 23rd Psalm was her comfort that night.

What discomforts are you facing this day? What struggles and pains are you wrestling with this night? Once in Royal David's City, the Great Shepherd, the Good Shepherd, the Chief Shepherd, and the True Shepherd, as God's Word says of Christ, was born. It may be the least used but the most appropriate Christmas greeting of all, but say it with me now and let it be your comfort: "The Lord *is* my shepherd, and that is enough."

In the Light of the Word
John MacArthur

THIS IS A HYMN FOR CHILDREN, reminding them that Christ is not only their Lord and Savior, but also their example. Stanza 3 closes with these words: "Christian children all must be mild, obedient, good as he."

The opening stanza sets forth the familiar features of the birth of God's Son— the city, the stable, the manger, the mother, and the Child. The second stanza is a reminder of the amazing condescension of Christ, who though He was "God and Lord of all" set aside His glory and "came down to earth from heaven." The stanza goes on to recite how His entrance into this world brought Him into inconceivable poverty and humility: "His shelter was a stable, and his cradle was a stall." Those humble beginnings set the course of His whole life and ministry—always among "the poor, and mean, and lowly" rather than among kings and celebrities.

The thought is an echo of 2 Corinthians 8:9: "Though He was rich, yet for your sakes He became poor, that you through His poverty might become rich" (cf. also Philippians 2:5-8).

The third stanza celebrates Christ's holy perfection even "through all his wondrous childhood." Scripture repeatedly emphasizes His utter sinlessness (Hebrews 4:15; 7:26; 1 Peter 2:22; 1 John 3:5). That necessarily means He was sinless even through His childhood and adolescent years. And thus He is the perfect example for all children who love Him.

As the hymn goes on, "that child so dear and gentle" has returned to "heav'n above." Having accomplished His saving work, He ascended to the Father's right hand in exaltation.

And thus the Christmas story as told in this hymn ends where it began—in heaven. Stanza 5 sings: "We shall see him, but in heaven, set at God's right hand on high."

Think of it: In heaven we will actually see the Lord face to face. That is impossible in the earthly realm. After all, God said, "No man shall see Me, and live" (Exodus 33:20). John 1:18 and 1 John 4:12 both say, "No one has seen God at any time." First Timothy 6:16 declares that God "alone has immortality, dwelling in unapproachable light, whom no man has seen or can see." As long as we are tainted by sin, we cannot stand in the presence of God. The view of such perfect righteousness would destroy us.

God is therefore inaccessible to mortal man on a face-to-face basis. That is what made Christ's incarnation so wonderful. Although no man has ever seen God at any time,

The only begotten Son, who is in the bosom of the Father, He has declared Him.
—JOHN 1:18

God "became flesh and dwelt among us, and we beheld His glory, the glory as of the only begotten of the Father" (John 1:14). He came to our world to dwell among us, and one day He will take all who trust Him to heaven, where they will dwell with Father, Son, and Holy Spirit in perfect fellowship. What a breathtaking reality!

In heaven, since we will be free from sin, we will finally see God's glory unveiled in its fullness. That will be a more pleasing, spectacular sight than anything we have known or could ever imagine on earth.

This has always been the deepest longing of the redeemed soul. The psalmist said,

As the deer pants for the water brooks,
So pants my soul for You, O God.
My soul thirsts for God, for the living God.
When shall I come and appear before God?

—PSALM 42:1-2

And Philip, speaking for all the disciples, said to Christ, "Lord, show us the Father, and it is sufficient for us" (John 14:8).

Revelation 22:3-4 seals the promise: "The throne of God and of the Lamb shall be in it, and His servants shall serve Him. *They shall see His face*" (emphasis added). "Crowned all in white," they shall worship Him forever.

FROM OUT OF THE PAST
Bobbie Wolgemuth

CECIL FRANCES ALEXANDER, a remarkable Irish woman, used all the skill of her privileged childhood to help common children understand some of the deeper doctrines of faith. As the daughter of an English army officer, she was exposed to both English and Irish aristocracy. She was single until the age of thirty-two and wrote many verses and poems during those years, especially for children.

It was her love of poetry and young people that helped her paint word pictures in hymns like "All Things Bright and Beautiful." It was in verse that she was able to give her young listeners vivid descriptions of God's creativity.

Each little flow'r that opens,
Each little bird that sings,
He made their glowing colors,
He made their tiny wings.

She used the same method of simple verse in "Once in Royal David's City" to teach essential doctrines of the Christian faith to the young and the young at heart. The children of the Victorian era were taken to both morning and evening church services in cold, austere structures. Under the stern and sometimes droning voice of the rector, they were taught essential biblical doctrine. They dared not so much wiggle or make noise while they sat on wooden benches in this solemn setting.

Knowing that every child was tediously required to learn church catechism inspired Cecil to publish fourteen hymns, which appeared in the book *Hymns for Little Children*. Each hymn explained a different portion of the Apostles' Creed. This Christmas carol began as a means to employ the imagination of the children and to grasp the significance of the little baby, "Jesus Christ . . . born of the Virgin Mary."

In addition to teaching the Creed, Mrs. Alexander moralizes in the third verse, helping the children to see young Jesus as a model boy. She emphasizes that "Christian children all must be mild, obedient, good as he."

It was during this era that the church needed to respond to the unusually high infant mortality rate. Due to epidemics, inadequate health facilities, and poor living conditions, it was not unusual to see tiny coffins on crude farm wagons followed by mourners. When a death occurred, the bell tolled from the tower—the little bell for an infant, the heavy one for adults. Against this sorrowing, Cecil addressed the need for the children to visualize where this little one they so loved would go. She assures them that "he leads his children on to the place where he is gone" and paints a poetic epitaph of the little ones as "stars[,] his children crowned all in white."

Cecil Alexander filled her life with helping children. She was instrumental in founding a school for the deaf and left a rich legacy of poetic teaching for those she loved. With tenderness and poetry she led the little ones she loved to the throne of God, where all their eyes at last would see Him.

Angels We Have Heard on High

JAMES CHADWICK
1813-1882

Angels we have heard on high, sweetly singing o'er the plains,
And the mountains in reply echo back their joyous strains.
Gloria in excelsis Deo, gloria in excelsis Deo.

Shepherds, why this jubilee? Why your joyous strains prolong?
Say what may the tidings be, which inspire your heav'nly song?
Gloria in excelsis Deo, gloria in excelsis Deo.

Come to Bethlehem and see him whose birth the angels sing;
Come, adore on bended knee Christ the Lord, the newborn King.
Gloria in excelsis Deo, gloria in excelsis Deo.

At the Heart of the Hymn

Joni Eareckson Tada

৶

Glory to God in the highest, and on earth peace to men on whom his favor rests.

— Luke 2:14

The maple-walled music room of Woodlawn Senior High School vibrated as the school choir lustfully and loudly—very loudly—belted out the refrain, "Glo - - - - - ri-a in excelsis Deo!" There wasn't a kid in the choir who didn't have his or her eyes closed, head back, singing his or her part at the top of his or her lungs. After all, everyone loved this soul-stirring refrain. It may well be the most fun to sing of any carol at Christmas!

"Hold it, everybody . . ." Mr. Blackwell rapped his wooden baton on the piano top. "I said *Hold it!*" he demanded. Basses and altos, sopranos and tenors trailed off, their various parts winding down and heading off-pitch, finally crash-landing to a halt. "Someone in the alto section. Second row. You, Eareckson!" He pointed his baton at me.

I couldn't help it. I loved the song too much. I was just having way too much fun with all the wonderful runs in the first three measures. All those eighth notes, jammed together, begging to be sung like an opera star would in *La Boheme*.

Mr. Blackwell tapped his baton on his palm. "Miss Eareckson, you are not the primo alto here. You are supposed to *support* the melody, my dear, not drown it out." The kids around me giggled.

"Hey, we'll take you in the tenor section," Jay Leverton said. "We need big girls with big voices." "Just shut up, you guys," someone in the altos jeered. There was more laughter. Somebody threw a wad of paper.

"Okay, enough!" Mr. Blackwell grabbed control before more paper started flying. He tapped the baton—everyone got quiet—raised his hands, nodded at the pianist, glared at me, and then with a 1-2-3-4 on the downbeat, our choir launched once again into "Angels We Have Heard on High." This time I was careful to support my soprano friends, saving the mezzo-soprano Brunhild-in-the-Viking-cap thing for another day.

Some of my favorite Christmas memories were given birth in that choir room. We were only high school kids, but James Blackwell—bless his soul—opened our ears, eyes, and hearts to a whole world of classical music for choir. Standing in the alto section, halfway up the theater-like room, I was surrounded by sound, in the middle of the melody, lost in the harmony, and lifted by the happy-hearted unity that only a choir member feels in the midst of singing a great chorus with eighty others. I had a part to play, and it felt wonderful.

Funny thing is, I don't imagine that more than a handful of us kids really knew what we were singing about. But truth is truth, whether declared by a believer or an unbeliever. And I believe the words to this awesome and ancient carol were used of God to prepare my heart to receive the Savior. It was to be a year later that I would personally ascribe to Christ all that the angels heralded in this carol.

Thirty-five years have passed since my days of high school choir. Last year at our Joni and Friends Christmas party, we closed our evening together with an impromptu singing of "Angels We Have Heard on High." Most of us are in our fifties, and we've sung this song by heart countless times.

But the kid in me squeezed out when we got to the first bar of eighth notes. Once again I was at the New York Metropolitan Opera House with a shield in one hand and a spear in the other, blonde braids and all, belting it out for all it was worth . . .

"Gloria in excelsis Deo!"

In the Light of the Word

John MacArthur

HE ANNOUNCEMENT OF THE ANGELS to the shepherds is the theme of this hymn. In fact, the Latin chorus "Gloria in excelsis Deo" (literally, "Glory to God in the highest") borrows the very words that the shepherds heard outside Bethlehem.

Angels played a critical role in revealing the coming of the Savior to humanity. First, it was an angel sent by God to Zacharias the priest to tell him that his barren wife, Elizabeth, would have a son who would be the forerunner of Israel's long-awaited Messiah (Luke 1:5-20).

That staggering announcement broke 400 years of God's silence. It had been an even longer time since anyone had knowingly been visited by an angel.

Next was the angel Gabriel who came with the Word of God to Mary, telling her that she would be the mother of God's Son (Luke 1:26-37). It was probably also Gabriel who came to Joseph to tell him what God had done in Mary (Matthew 1:20).

When Jesus was born, an angel of the Lord appeared to the shepherds, telling them the good news of "Christ the Lord, the newborn King" (see Luke 2:8-11). Then all heaven broke loose! "Suddenly there was with the angel a multitude of the heavenly host praising God and saying: 'Glory to God in the highest'" (Luke 2:13-14). The word "host" is from a Greek word used to describe a military encampment. Christ also used military imagery to describe angels in Matthew 26:53 ("legions of angels"). Revelation 5:11 suggests that there is an angelic number too large to count.

At this point in the Nativity narrative, we come to the transcendent pinnacle of all thought and action—giving God glory for the giving of His Son and our Savior!

Here is a rare look at heavenly worship—a glimpse of what holy angels *always* do. In this case, the angels were praising God for the incarnation of His Son in order to save sinners.

Glorifying God is the cherished duty and highest privilege of all rational beings—and particularly giving Him glory for His redeeming grace. This is what occupies saints and angels forever (as the scene in Revelation 4—5 illustrates).

"In excelsis" ("the highest") refers to heaven. Those angels spoke on behalf of all heaven when they glorified God.

The familiar phrase of Luke 2:14—"on earth peace, goodwill toward men!"—is better rendered as the *New American Standard Bible* translates it: "on earth peace among men with whom He is pleased." It limits God's peace to the people of God's good pleasure—His elect. This is profound and compelling theology. Rarely is a raging debate on theology settled by the words of angels, but here is one. How does salvation come to sinners? Is it the sinner who chooses God because it pleases him to do so? Or is it God who chooses sinners because it pleases Him to do so? The answer of the holy angels in heaven is the latter. God's peace is not a reward for human merit, but a gracious gift from God to those whom He is well-pleased to save for the display of His own glory and grace. Peace with God belongs to those whom God is eternally pleased to save. And He saves whom and when He chooses.

In other words, the angels do not glorify God for the will of men who choose Him, but for the grace of God who chose them and the wisdom and power of God to reconcile them to Himself. This directs us to the sovereign, gracious, eternal decree and will of God, by which before the creation of the world (and thus not on the merit or deserving of any sinners) He chose to save some sinners.

That is why the psalmist wrote:

> *Not unto us, O LORD, not unto us, but to Your name give glory, because of Your mercy, because of Your truth.*
>
> —PSALM 115:1

And the coming of "him whose birth the angels sing" was for the purpose of bringing eternal honor and praise from saints and angels to God because He was pleased to save sinners.

"Gloria in excelsis Deo."

FROM OUT OF THE PAST
Bobbie Wolgemuth

ALTHOUGH WE KNOW VERY LITTLE about the origin of the music to this familiar hymn, we do know that the French tune used to carry the lilting angel voices is full of movement and vitality. It was common in the 1700s in Europe to hear people caroling through the streets and stopping at the homes of friends to share goodwill and celebration.

Originally the carols had nothing to do with Christmas but were associated with festivities that included circling dances and dramatic performances to celebrate the end of winter and the promise of spring. Singers and actors traveling throughout the countryside performing in the streets captured the imagination of the villagers. It is easy to see why the medieval church adapted some of the tunes for use in Easter and Christmas commemoration. Latin words from the staid litanies were added to popular tunes of the day and incorporated into the services. "Gloria in excelsis Deo" may have been added in this manner to the traditional French melody to give choir members the same lively rolling spirit we enjoy today.

It is interesting that the Anglican Church and later Puritan zealots strongly denounced the singing of many of these spirited carols due to the pagan associations. The bands of traveling entertainers often sang near pubs or outside homes where their "wassailing" became boisterous and rude. The church could not tolerate the approval of such levity and announced that there should be no figured music in church anthems. It continued to be an intense battle for the Reformers who wanted the people singing in church, not just on their own balconies. They directed believers to "sing all, sing lustily, sing in time, and above all, sing spiritually." Perhaps this carol remained popular because it was filled with word pictures that lifted the singers to look high and sing sweetly with jubilee and joyous strains. It is probably why our own feet want to dance when we sing it!

Come, Thou Long-Expected Jesus

CHARLES WESLEY

1707-1788

Come, thou long-expected Jesus, born to set thy people free;
From our fears and sins release us; let us find our rest in thee.
Israel's strength and consolation, hope of all the earth thou art,
Dear Desire of ev'ry nation, joy of ev'ry longing heart.

Born thy people to deliver, born a child and yet a king,
Born to reign in us forever, now thy gracious kingdom bring.
By thine own eternal Spirit rule in all our hearts alone;
By thine all-sufficient merit, raise us to thy glorious throne.

At the Heart of the Hymn

Robert Wolgemuth

&

As the deer pants for streams of water,

so my soul pants for you, O God.

My soul thirsts for God,

for the living God.

—Psalm 42:1-2a

Before he was my dad, Samuel Wolgemuth was a hunter. I've held the evidence in my hand—sepia-toned, black-and-white photos, curling with age. There's my dad, shotgun slung over his left shoulder and a dead pheasant in his right hand.

My siblings and I never got the chance to see our dad hunt because soon after they were married, our mother put an end to it. I'm sure she did this graciously, but the ultimatum was pretty simple: "Hunt or be a father." Lucky for us, he stopped hunting.

Please believe me—I don't have a problem with hunters or hunting. I have uncles, cousins, and friends who almost live for hunting season. And I've sat at their tables and enjoyed the bounty of their sharpshooting. It's just that hunting wasn't *our* family's thing. Now you know why.

Because of this, instead of providing us with target practice, deer have been a kind of family art form. I can still hear my mother's gasps as we drove through the Pennsylvania countryside. "Look over there . . . a deer!" Our dad would slow the car, and our hearts would race. There she was, a deer, sleek and exquisite against the seamless backdrop of a verdant meadow. With the sound of our car, she would bound into the woods, her white tail following her into the dark and protective cover of the deep thicket.

We would "oooh" and "aaah."

Just a few weeks ago, I heard a man ask, "Have you ever seen a fat deer?" I laughed at the image, then quickly reviewed more than five decades of deer watching. "Come to think of it," I said, "I've never seen a fat deer."

"Do you know why?" my friend continued, not waiting for my response. "It's because a deer's longings are completely satisfied at the stream."

My friend, a veritable repository of extraordinary information, continued to talk. But I was no longer listening. I was having another one of those deer-sighting, heart-racing moments.

God has placed in the heart of a deer the need for the brook. Once he's had a drink, he is satisfied. It is enough.

And God has placed in our hearts the need for . . . Himself. It's a longing that cannot be pacified with anything *but* Himself.

We try to fill this longing with other things—even "good" things—but they do not satisfy. Intellectually, we may give in to the truth of this, but the enticement of these replacements still draws us in. As a result there *are* overweight . . . and depressed and anxious and angry and frustrated . . . humans. People like you and me, longing for God.

The apostle Paul's words should ring in our ears.

> *For in Christ the fullness of the Deity lives in bodily form, and you have been given fullness in Christ.*
>
> —COLOSSIANS 2:9-10A

Complete. Satisfied. Enough. "Come, thou long-expected Jesus." What a great Christmas present for someone who has *almost* everything.

IN THE LIGHT OF THE WORD

John MacArthur

୧୨

TRULY THE SAVIOR HAD BEEN "long-expected." He was the One whom God would send, in the words of this hymn, "to set thy people free." He was the One for whom the faithful of Israel were earnestly watching.

The hymn is filled with biblical allusions about this messianic expectation, including: "Israel's strength and consolation" (see Luke 2:25) and "Desire of every nation" (see Haggai 2:7). Those and other messianic promises had the people of God expectantly awaiting the coming One they longed for so desperately.

From the first promise of God to fallen sinners that the offspring of a woman would crush Satan's head, all true believers had hoped for His birth. The first intimation of a sacrificial Savior came in the act of God, who (for the first time in history) killed an animal to provide a covering for the shamed couple (Genesis 3:15, 21). All the Old Testament sacrifices—together with the promises, types, images, and prophecies—prefigured a Redeemer. As the promises multiplied, the hope of God's people grew stronger and stronger.

He was not only "Israel's strength and consolation"—He was the "hope of all the earth"—the only Savior for all of humanity. In the words of Scripture, He would be "the Savior of the world" (John 4:42; 1 John 4:14). Whether they realized it or not, He was the "joy of ev'ry longing heart."

This hymn celebrates a number of paradoxes associated with the coming of Christ. He whose glories never end set aside that glory and came to earth to bear our sin and sadness. Therefore "we do not have a High Priest who cannot sympathize with our weaknesses" (Hebrews 4:15). And, paradox upon paradox, because He tasted our sadness—including the sadness of death—by His life He brings us salvation and joy.

Leaving behind the riches of heaven, He was born in a manger. The outward appearance of His lowly estate is yet another paradox. He was "born a child and yet a king." More than that, here is unspeakable, everlasting wonder: Born as a human infant, He is nevertheless Lord of all.

Those very paradoxes explain why so few in Israel recognized their Messiah at His birth. Although He was "long-expected" by multitudes of believers, they expected Him to come in glory, not clothed in such humility. They anticipated a powerful, conquering ruler, not a simple carpenter's son. They were prepared for Him to restore the glory of David's kingdom; they were not anticipating a child so poor that He would be born in a manger.

One man in all of Israel, the aged and godly Simeon, personified wonderfully the expectant remnant of Jews. Simeon's hope was coupled with a true faith, and by God's grace his eyes were opened to see that this unassuming Child was indeed the long-expected Savior of Israel.

Simeon is described in Luke's Gospel:

> *Behold, there was a man in Jerusalem whose name was Simeon, and this man was just and devout, waiting for the Consolation of Israel, and the Holy Spirit was upon him. And it had been revealed to him by the Holy Spirit that he would not see death before he had seen the Lord's Christ.*
>
> —LUKE 2:25-26

With that information from God, no doubt the old man lived in almost feverish anticipation, waking every day with the hope that it would be that day of days when he would see Messiah. Finally that hope became reality. Led by the

Holy Spirit, he went to the temple to worship. And on that day, "the parents brought in the Child Jesus" (v. 27).

Scripture does not say how Simeon recognized the infant as "Israel's strength and consolation," but he did.

> *He took him up in his arms and blessed God and said: "Lord, now You are letting Your servant depart in peace, according to Your word; for my eyes have seen Your salvation."*
>
> —*vv. 28-30*

In the words of the prophet Isaiah,

> *"Behold, this is our God;*
> *We have waited for Him, and He will save us.*
> *This is the LORD; we have waited for Him;*
> *we will be glad and rejoice in His salvation."*
>
> —*25:9*

FROM OUT OF THE PAST

Bobbie Wolgemuth

KNOWN AS THE HYMN-WRITER WHO "set the masses to singing," Charles Wesley along with his brother John also set the world on fire with the ideas that were later called Methodism. It is impossible to talk about the incredible accomplishments of this writer of over 6,500 hymns without looking at the powerful foundation laid for his work at the schoolhouse of his mother's knee.

Susanna Wesley knew that Charles and in fact all nineteen of her children carried a promise with them, a hidden treasure that had to be led through biblical education and a hospitable home. As a homeschooler, Susanna from the earliest years let them read their first lessons from the Bible. She mingled the name of Jesus with their ABC's as she drew out their infant minds with discipline and scholarship. When Charles was only five years old, his mother wrote a letter to her husband, Samuel, who was away on a trip: "I cannot but look upon every soul you leave under my care as a talent committed to me under a trust by the great Lord of all the families both of heaven and earth. And if I am unfaithful to Him or you in neglecting to improve these talents, how shall I answer when He shall command me to render an account of my stewardship?"

Her creativity in mothering led her to zealously promote reading and biblical instruction every day along with the simple singing of psalms. Her passion for prayer led her to pray fervently each day for and with the children. She still found time to enter her own "prayer closet" with nineteen children close by. Throwing her apron up over her face, she managed to close herself up with Jesus in the darkness of the fabric.

Susanna's desire was to "take more than ordinary care for their souls"; so discipline was woven into their daily lives. She wrote, "In order to form the minds of children, the first thing to be done is to conquer their will. When the will of a child is totally subdued, and it is brought to revere and stand in awe of the parents, then a great many follies may be passed by. This is the only strong and rational foundation of a religious education. As self-will is the root of all sin and misery, whatever checks it promotes their future happiness and piety. Religion is nothing else than doing the will of God, and not our own."

It was at home with Susanna that Charles learned a passion for ministry. After hosting visiting missionaries, she wrote, "I was inspired that I might pray more, speak with more warmth of affection, and I resolved to start with my own children. I take such a portion of time as I can spare every night to discourse with each child apart." Charles's appointed day was Saturday.

The family prepared for the many visitors that would come to their cottage on Sunday for a simple service of hymn singing, Bible study, and prayer. Charles observed a type of group interaction that was the blueprint destined to become the Wesleyan Revival in all of Europe and the Americas. Perhaps Susanna sensed the enormous capacity of those Saturdays with Charles. Her hopes were multiplied beyond her highest expectations, and today we enjoy the legacy of her diligent parenting every time we sing one of the more than 6,500 hymns and eighteen Christmas carols that Charles wrote. Her life verse may well have been, "No eye has seen, no ear has heard, no mind has conceived what God has prepared for those who love him" (1 Corinthians 2:9).

What Child Is This

WILLIAM CHATTERTON DIX
1837-1898

What child is this, who, laid to rest, on Mary's lap is sleeping?

Whom angels greet with anthems sweet,

while shepherds watch are keeping?

This, this is Christ the King,

whom shepherds guard and angels sing:

Haste, haste to bring him laud, the babe, the son of Mary.

Why lies he in such mean estate, where ox and ass are feeding?

Good Christian, fear; for sinners here the silent Word is pleading.

Nails, spear, shall pierce him through: the cross be borne for me, for you:

Hail, hail the Word made flesh, the babe, the son of Mary.

So bring him incense, gold, and myrrh; come, peasant, king, to own him;

The King of kings salvation brings, let loving hearts enthrone him.

Raise, raise the song on high, the virgin sings her lullaby:

Joy, joy for Christ is born, the babe, the son of Mary.

At the Heart of the Hymn

Joni Eareckson Tada

Where is the one who has been born king of the Jews?

—Matthew 2:2

As an artist, I love learning new techniques, and I will never forget the first time my art coach, Jim Sewell, had me draw a human figure using live models. I wanted to render a picture of Mary holding Baby Jesus, and so I invited my girlfriend with her neighbor's baby into my studio. We dressed her in peasant garb, after which Jim took special pains to pose her just so. He then carefully placed her sleeping baby in her arms. Jim stepped back, I grabbed my pencil in my mouth, and I started hurriedly sketching before the infant boy woke up.

Jim whispered instructions as I sketched. "Notice how his little cheek pouches against the woman's arm . . . see if you can catch that." "Don't miss these little details—the way a newborn's hair looks soft and fuzzy," he said, artfully cupping his hands around the child's head.

After I got my sketches and my friend left with the baby, Jim and I started flipping through anatomy books, examining the structure of a baby's skull. "Notice how much forehead an infant has . . . it's not like a three- or four-year-old's." I must confess, I had never noticed that feature before. "And look at where the placement of the ears are."

Within a week, my studio wall was covered with photos of infants, sketches, anatomy charts, and color tests. I had learned that, yes, even the flesh tones of newborn infants require extra rose tones.

A month later, my pastel pencil rendering was complete. And a month later, I was still marveling that the God of the universe poured Himself into *baby flesh*. We've seen so many paintings of Baby Jesus looking like an icon or a plaster-of-paris statue, sometimes with a halo, sometimes not, sometimes holding a globe and scepter, other times looking off into some other world with the eyes of a sage, that we forget He had tiny capillaries and little fingernails, a heart rate and a runny nose, that He urped and squirmed and breathed abdominally.

The God who set suns and stars spinning in motion, who carved out rivers and ladled out seas, who dreamed up time and space, this God was *born*. Astounding! As incredible as fitting an oil tanker into an oil can or a battleship into a bathtub. God became flesh. His little cheek pouched against His mother's arm . . . His newborn hair was soft and fuzzy . . . the forehead was wide and high, like any infant's . . . His ears were set low . . . And even though Middle-Eastern, His skin was rosy.

"What child is this?" A child, demurely divine. Wholly Spirit. But also a child made from dust, flesh, bone, and blood. One hundred percent God . . . one hundred percent man. We are amazed that God the Son would become a man, but equally astounding is that a man or woman can become a son or daughter of God. The Nativity is a holy story, but also *human*.

And it's been told thousands of times. Humanly speaking, a busy innkeeper hurriedly growls there's no vacancy, then slams the door shut in Joseph's face. Joseph stands outside in the cold, listening to the laughter behind the door, wondering where in the world—*how* in this world—he will find a bed for his wife that night. He turns, slightly bewildered, and without a word leads Mary to the stable. Lifting her gently from the donkey, he helps her to a small bed of straw in an empty stall. A young bride goes into labor, a new husband nervously attends, and while music and feasting continue behind the warm walls of the inn, yards away the Son of God quietly slips into history. Human history.

"What child is this?" He is God, warm and alive, close and sweet as an infant's breath.

IN THE LIGHT OF THE WORD

John MacArthur

◦◦

HIS TRADITIONAL ENGLISH CAROL asks one of the most important questions ever to confront the human mind. "What think ye of Christ? whose son is he?" (Matthew 22:42, KJV). Who is the baby "on Mary's lap . . . sleeping"? Who is this One "whom angels greet with anthems sweet, while shepherds watch are keeping"?

The answers often proposed to that question are myriad. Some have said He was a good and wise teacher. But good and wise teachers do not claim to be the God of the universe.

Some say He was a classic example of human virtue. But good examples don't spend their time with prostitutes, drunkards, dirty politicians, and social riffraff.

Some say He was a religious madman. But delusional minds and self-styled religious leaders don't speak the clear, profound, gracious words He spoke—nor do they offer up their lives for others.

Some think He was a deliberate deceiver. But a deceiver who died would stay dead.

Some say He was only a myth and that the whole story is just a legend. But myths don't set the calendar for all of human history.

"What child is this?" The carol answers, "This, this is Christ the King." King of what? "King of kings." Lord of all. The very God of the universe.

As so many of these Christmas carols remind us, this king was "the Word made flesh, the babe, the Son of Mary."

"Why lies he in such mean [lowly] estate, where ox and ass are feeding?" He had set aside His heavenly glory.

[He] made Himself of no reputation, taking the form of a bondservant, and coming in the likeness of men.

—PHILIPPIANS 2:7

Moreover,

Being found in appearance as a man, He humbled Himself and became obedient to the point of death, even the death of the cross.

—v. 8

In other words, unlike every other king, He deliberately came in the most abject humility, and with a purpose that at first glance seems unbefitting one of such eternal glory. He became flesh so that "nails, spear, shall pierce him through."

The hymn pictures Him already undertaking His priestly work as He lay in the manger: "Good Christian, fear; for sinners here the silent Word is pleading." That accords well with the truth of Hebrews 7:25: "Therefore He is also able to save to the uttermost those who come to God through Him, since He always lives to make intercession for them."

Stanza 3 is a call to worship that reminds us of the Magi who brought Him gifts in His infancy: "So bring Him incense, gold, and myrrh." The magi were pagan philosophers and occult practitioners who attended the kings of the East, especially in Persia and Assyria.

It is one of the great ironies of the Christmas story that while Christ's own people in the nation of Israel for the most part utterly ignored His birth and missed His significance, divine grace was drawing these Gentile wise men to recognize and worship Him. Thus God signified that the salvation brought by Israel's Messiah was for the whole world.

"Come, peasant, king, to own him," the carol pleads. This echoes the words of the apostle Paul, who commands us to pray for the salvation of "all men, [including] kings and all who are in authority. For this is good and acceptable in the sight of God our Savior, who desires all men to be saved and to come to the knowledge of the truth" (1 Timothy 2:1-4).

Those who hated Christ and ultimately put Him to death put a sign over His head as He hung on the cross, indicating the crime for which He was being tortured and executed. It read: "THIS IS JESUS THE KING OF THE JEWS" (Matthew 27:37). That was only part of the truth. He is the eternal King of both Jews and Gentiles. Truly His kingdom is not of this world! We who believe are part of that kingdom where "loving hearts enthrone him."

FROM OUT OF THE PAST

Bobbie Wolgemuth

AS A LAYMAN AND ENGLISH-BORN son of a surgeon, William Chatterton Dix wrote many hymns and the words of this familiar carol. Although born in Bristol, England, his years of profitable business were mostly spent in Glasgow, Scotland, where he was a successful insurance salesman.

As every good peddler knows, you have to close the sale. And William included an appeal in most of his hymns for the singer to make a decision to move closer to a holy life. You can hear the plea in another Christmas hymn he wrote, "As With Gladness Men of Old." He calls us to join the wise men in a similar visit to the mercy seat.

As with joyful steps they sped,
To that lowly cradle-bed,
There to bend the knee before,

Him whom heav'n and earth adore;
So may we with willing feet
Ever seek thy mercy seat.

William was a prolific writer as a young twenty-something man. His hymns, however, were not born from "gladness." In his early twenties William became bedridden with a serious illness. Confined to bed, instead of his days being filled with activity and personal contacts, the lad struggled with depression.

It was this experience that led him to meet God in a deeper way and to pen some of his most artistic poetry. Being himself laid to rest, William knew it was for his *own* benefit that the "silent Word" was pleading. This brought hope to William's young heart and gave him renewed delight as he wrote "Joy, joy, for Christ is born, the babe, the son of Mary."

Perhaps it was the most productive sales presentation he ever made to triumphantly declare to his own hurting heart that "This, this is Christ the King."

The tune adapted to "What Child Is This" was the traditional "Greensleeves," which dates back to the sixteenth century. Although its authorship is sometimes attributed to Henry VII of England, it is probably an ancient Italian dance melody. Traveling bands of entertainers that moved throughout the countryside and various towns used the common melody. Variations of the tune were adapted in several countries all over Europe.

Some of the text has come into question in recent years by modernists who are uncomfortable with references to the phrase "the Word made flesh," coming from the first chapter of John's Gospel. The same criticisms have been directed to references to "peasant," "king," and "virgin."

Believers would do well to memorize the words as we know them today before more adjustments are made to the original truth. The babe was Jesus Christ, born of the Virgin Mary, and He was and is incarnate God! May our "loving hearts enthrone him"!

O Come, O Come, Emmanuel

JOHN MASON NEALE
1818-1866

HENRY S. COFFIN
1877-1954

O come, O come, Emmanuel, and ransom captive Israel,
That mourns in lonely exile here, until the Son of God appear.
Rejoice! Rejoice! Emmanuel shall come to thee, O Israel.

O come, O come, thou Lord of might, who to thy tribes, on Sinai's height,
In ancient times didst give the law in cloud and majesty and awe.
Rejoice! Rejoice! Emmanuel shall come to thee, O Israel.

O come, thou Rod of Jesse, free thine own from Satan's tyranny;
From depths of hell thy people save,
and give them vict'ry o'er the grave.
Rejoice! Rejoice! Emmanuel shall come to thee, O Israel.

O come, thou Dayspring from on high, and cheer us by thy drawing nigh;
Disperse the gloomy clouds of night, and death's dark shadows put to flight.
Rejoice! Rejoice! Emmanuel shall come to thee, O Israel.

O come, thou Key of David, come and open wide our heav'nly home;
Make safe the way that leads on high, and close the path to misery.
Rejoice! Rejoice! Emmanuel shall come to thee, O Israel.

At the Heart of the Hymn

Joni Eareckson Tada

∼

Nevertheless, there will be no more gloom for those who were in distress. In the past he humbled the land of Zebulun and the land of Naphtali, but in the future he will honor Galilee of the Gentiles, by the way of the sea, along the Jordan.

— Isaiah 9:1

If it's the First Sunday in Advent, you will most likely find me visiting the Episcopal church of my friend Judy. It's a little church up the road sweetly nestled against a hill overlooking the Conejo Valley. For a new church in this part of Southern California, it's quite unusual. It has an actual steeple! Candlelight bathes the sanctuary in an inviting glow, and the voices of the choir echo off the vaulted ceiling and concrete floor. If it weren't a balmy 75 degrees outside, I'd say I was in England.

Sunday service starts with the Collect. I can't think of a better way to begin the Christmas season than to turn to page 85 in *The Book of Common Prayer* and read, "Almighty God, give us grace that we may cast away the works of darkness." After that, a hymn is sung, usually "O Come, O Come, Emmanuel."

O come, thou Dayspring from on high,
And cheer us by thy drawing nigh;
Disperse the gloomy clouds of night,
And death's dark shadows put to flight.

After harmonizing on that bittersweet, almost wistful hymn in its minor key, there is the usual reading from the Old Testament. For the first week of Advent, that means Isaiah 1:1-20.

> *Ah, sinful nation, a people loaded with guilt, a brood of evildoers, children given to corruption! They have forsaken the LORD; they have spurned the Holy One of Israel and turned their backs on him. . . . When you spread out your hands in prayer, I will hide my eyes from you; even if you offer many prayers, I will not listen. Your hands are full of blood; wash and make yourselves clean. Take your evil deeds out of my sight! Stop doing wrong.*
>
> — ISAIAH 1:4, 15-16

Wait a minute. Stop the countdown to December 25th. Why all the gloomy images? A people loaded with guilt? A brood of evildoers? Prayers of supplication to cast away works of darkness? Many would say that's an odd way to drum up the Christmas spirit. Shouldn't we be decking the halls with boughs of holly and fa-la-la-ing? Getting into the holiday mood with yuletide cheer?

Sure, but don't worry. There will be plenty of weeks leading up to Christmas Day to celebrate with parties and glad-hearted carols. But it's appropriate on the First Sunday in Advent to first consider *why* the coming of Christ is happily heralded. How can we rejoice in the coming of the promised Savior unless we understand what we are being saved *from*?

And this is why I love this beautiful and ancient Christmas hymn. I know the ways of my heart. I know how easily I can get swept up into the glib glitter of the season. I need the concrete reminders of convicting Scriptures and songs in the key of A minor to rein in my heart. If no Savior were born, I'd still be lost, helpless, and hopeless! So when I sing this hymn in its haunting key, it's a way of telling my heart, "There's no Christmas spirit unless first there's the spirit of repentance. And don't forget it, Joni."

Maybe you feel your life can be sung in a minor key today. If so, you have a friend in this hymn. The words go on to include a triumphant chorus that echoes:

Rejoice! Rejoice!
Emmanuel shall come to thee, O Israel.

There's many a First Sunday in Advent when I've come out of that little Episcopal church, breathed the sweet, fresh air of December in California, and rejoiced! Emmanuel—God is with us! Praise the Lord—a Savior has come!

And what do you know . . . I'm in the *real* Christmas spirit!

IN THE LIGHT OF THE WORD
John MacArthur

THE LYRICS OF THIS BELOVED HYMN express the vast drama of redemption from the ancient covenant promises to the eternal consummation of our heavenly home. It gives such a breathtaking panorama of redemption that it is hard to take it all in without a long and careful look.

The hymn describes the plight of the sinner with dramatic and vivid imagery. The sinner is pictured as "captive," mourning, "lonely," exiled, in bondage to "Satan's tyranny," held by a frail thread of life over the gaping "depths of hell," doomed to "the grave," living under "the gloomy clouds of [sin's] night" and "death's dark shadows," and condemned to walk "the path of misery." All of that bleak and woeful language is sung to a tune set in a minor key, suggesting a dirge or a lament.

But it is more than that. It is a plaintive cry for Israel's Deliverer, the promised Messiah. A different name for Him is invoked at the beginning of each stanza. The hymn-writer borrows these from a catalog of Isaiah's best-known messianic prophecies.

In the first stanza, He is called "Emmanuel," after the prophecy of Isaiah 7:14. Matthew, who quotes Isaiah and gives the meaning of the name, celebrates the fulfillment of that prophecy at the birth of Christ.

> *Behold, the virgin shall be with child, and bear a Son, and they shall call His name Immanuel [God with us].*
>
> —*1:23*

In the second stanza, the Deliverer is called "Lord of might"—a reference to Isaiah 9:6, which designates Him as "Mighty God." That stresses His deity, His sovereignty, and His almighty power. The rest of the stanza underscores the fact of His deity by noting that He is Israel's Lawgiver.

Next he is called the "Rod of Jesse," borrowing prophetic imagery from Isaiah 11:1-5. That passage foretells the coming of Israel's Messiah as both Deliverer and righteous Judge. Jesse was David's father; so the title reminds us that Christ is heir to the Davidic throne.

In stanza 4, an amazing title for the Messiah is borrowed from a New Testament text: "Dayspring from on high." That expression comes from Zacharias' prophecy in Luke 1:78. Zacharias was a priest in Israel and father of the last prophet, John the Baptist. When John, the forerunner of the Messiah, was born, Zacharias praised God in a Spirit-inspired prophecy.

Zacharias' thoughts about the coming Messiah were all phrased in the language of the Old Testament covenants. The theme of Zacharias' praise and joy was exactly what this hymn pleads for—the salvation of the Lord in the Person of the promised Deliverer.

Zacharias said that the darkness and shadow of death would be dispelled by the tender mercy of God, who was sending the "Dayspring" or Sunrise. The word literally means "the rising." It refers to the first light of sunrise that scatters the darkness of night. It pictures the Messiah as "the Sun of Righteousness" (Malachi 4:2)—"the light of the world" (John 8:12). His coming would end the darkness of sin and death for His people.

But this, too, turns out to be another reference to Isaiah's messianic prophecies. Isaiah 9:2 says, "The people that walked in darkness have seen a great light: they that dwell in the land of the shadow of death, upon them hath the light shined" (KJV). The Dayspring from on High thus disperses the gloomy clouds of sin's dark night.

In the final stanza, "Key of David" once again refers to the One who has the right to David's throne. Isaiah 22:22 says, "The key of the house of David I will lay on his shoulder; so he shall open, and no one shall shut; and he shall shut, and no one shall open." That prophecy is echoed by Christ Himself in Revelation 3:7.

As the remainder of the stanza suggests, what is opened for Emmanuel's people is the way to heaven, and what is closed to them is the path to misery. Indeed, what He opens, no one can shut, and what He closes, no one can open.

FROM OUT OF THE PAST
Bobbie Wolgemuth

ANYONE WHO LOVES HUNTING FOR ANTIQUES has a lot in common with the translator of "Veni Emmanuel" ("O Come, O Come, Emmanuel"). The rediscovery of Latin and Greek hymn texts was the specialty of John Mason Neale. This prolific English scholar has given the modern church scores of ancient treasures in fine sacred hymn translations.

Brought up in a solid Christian home, John had a reawakening of his faith through the student movement at Oxford University. In his twenties, his passion for hymnology became his tool of evangelism. John was a master of translation and musical adaptation to make solemn, age-old liturgies useful to the Church. The first appearance of familiar hymns like "All Glory, Laud, and Honor" and "Of the Father's Love Begotten" were text lines woven from the antiquated bounty he found.

Neale struggled with poor health. Although frail of body, he continued to build up the Body of Christ through hymnology until his death at age forty-eight. In another Christmas translation, "Good Christian Men, Rejoice," he seems to rise above all problems with the simple admonition to rejoice "with heart and soul and voice." It could have been his own mortality that inspired the confident words "Now ye need not fear the grave: Jesus Christ was born to save!"

It seems that his passion for translating left him without wealth or a financial legacy. He spent the last years of his life surviving on less than fifty dollars a year. The investment he made with his lifework is secure within the pages of our hymnbooks. There is no appraisal high enough for its value.

O Little Town of Bethlehem

PHILLIPS BROOKS

1835-1893

O little town of Bethlehem, how still we see thee lie;
Above thy deep and dreamless sleep the silent stars go by:
Yet in thy dark streets shineth the everlasting Light;
The hopes and fears of all the years are met in thee tonight.

For Christ is born of Mary; and gathered all above,
While mortals sleep, the angels keep their watch of wond'ring love.
O morning stars, together proclaim the holy birth!
And praises sing to God the King, and peace to men on earth.

How silently, how silently, the wondrous gift is giv'n!
So God imparts to human hearts the blessings of his heav'n.
No ear may hear his coming, but in this world of sin,
Where meek souls will receive him still, the dear Christ enters in.

O holy child of Bethlehem, descend to us, we pray;
Cast out our sin and enter in; be born in us today.
We hear the Christmas angels the great glad tidings tell;
O come to us, abide with us, our Lord Emmanuel.

AT THE HEART OF THE HYMN
Robert Wolgemuth

༄

The Word became flesh and made his dwelling among us.

—JOHN 1:14A

There's no place like home.

—DOROTHY

UNTIL I WAS SEVENTEEN YEARS OLD I had never driven a nail. Oh, there were a few pathetic attempts at hammering when I built forts in the woods behind our house with the neighbor boys. That doesn't really count. But as a teenager, the wonderful world of building homes was about to burst on my heart.

During the summer between high school graduation and my first year in college, I got a job with a real construction company. Until that summer, I had no idea how thrilling the world of putting together homes was. I fell in love with the business.

Since that summer, I have driven thousands of nails. I've built and rebuilt homes for our family and lots of friends. A few years ago I even bought a compressor and a nail gun. Now I can drive nails with the simple squeeze of a trigger.

Do you know how important house-building is to God? Of course, you *know* that He's in the family-building business and the church-building business. But I'm not talking about that. I'm talking about real construction—the brick and mortar kind. God's in *that* business.

Way back in the Old Testament, God told Moses, ". . . have them make a sanctuary for me, and I will dwell among them" (Exodus 25:8). So Moses obediently strapped on his nail apron and built a building. And because the Israelites were on a perpetual road trip, he made God's home—the tabernacle—completely portable, as he had been instructed. From that moment forward, it has been God's design that His earthly home would be a visible structure. Centuries later, God designated King Solomon as the general contractor for the Israelites' permanent home for worship, the temple.

I love this Christmas carol because the setting is King David's hometown. Familiar buildings line the darkened streets. Everyone is sound asleep. Everyone that is, except angels, Mary, Joseph, a few shepherds, and the baby Jesus, God's new earthly and visible dwelling place.

Tucked inside this tiny body was the fullness of a holy and sovereign God. This baby boy, cooing in a feeding trough, had spoken billions of galaxies into existence with that very same voice. Jesus was God's home, and His plan was for us to long for this home.

A few months after starting my job with the contractor, I quit and went off to college as planned. In spite of being a young man with lots of independence and a future to prepare for, I remember the feeling that crept over me after just a few days. It was a sensation I had not known before—at least, not quite like this. Like a twelve-year-old away at summer camp, I became gravely homesick. I told no one. By late October, my case was terminal.

I hand-lettered a sign that said, "College student going home." I put on a tie and slipped a windbreaker over my head. Five hours later I was walking down my street. Spotting the split-level at the intersection of Park and Main, I broke into a dead run. This boy was home.

In the fullness of time, in the city of David, God fashioned a perfect dwelling place. He was "our Lord Emmanuel," and on this night He became the home we long for.

Is it any wonder that our hearts ache to be with Him at Christmas?

In the Light of the Word

John MacArthur

⨏

THE MAJOR FEATURE OF THIS HYMN is the emphatic identification of
Bethlehem as the chosen birthplace of Messiah, the One in whom "the hopes
and fears of all the years" were focused.

Bethlehem (Hebrew: "house of bread") is about five miles southwest of
Jerusalem, in the fertile hill country of Judah, cradled between two ridges and
located in the main highway from Jerusalem to Egypt. Its name came from the
grain produced there in Old Testament times, and it is an especially fitting name
for the place where the Bread of Life was born (cf. John 6:35).

Bethlehem is where Jacob buried Rachel (Genesis 35:19), where Ruth met
and married Boaz (Ruth 1:22; 2:4) and where their illustrious grandson, David,
grew up and tended sheep (1 Samuel 17:12-15).

The prophet Micah predicted that Bethlehem would be the birthplace of
Messiah:

> *But you, Bethlehem Ephrathah, though you are little among the thousands of
> Judah, yet out of you shall come forth to Me the One to be Ruler in Israel, whose
> goings forth are from of old, from everlasting.*
>
> —5:2

"Ephrathah" ("fruitful") differentiates this Bethlehem from a Galilean town
with the same name. In New Testament times Bethlehem of Judea was known
for its vineyards and olive trees. It was small but greatly honored because David,
Israel's greatest king, had been born there. Micah says that although Bethlehem
was "little" relative to other cities in Judah, the Messiah would come from that

town—"the One to be Ruler in Israel." And Micah joins the constant biblical theme of the Christmas story—that the child born to be Messiah and Ruler was none other than the eternal God, whose "goings forth are from long ago, from everlasting."

The prophecy of Micah is thus one of the clearest, most unassailable testimonies to the messiahship of Jesus Christ, who was a son of David both through His father's line (Matthew 1:1-17) and through His mother's (Luke 3:23-38).

It may not have been completely accurate for Phillips Brooks to imagine Bethlehem at the birth of Jesus Christ with the words "how still we see thee lie" and resting "silently" in "deep and dreamless sleep." After all, the town was bursting with crowds there to register for the census. It was so crowded that no room was available for Joseph and Mary (Luke 2:7). Nonetheless, most in the town were utterly oblivious to the magnitude of the event that was occurring in their midst.

Unknown to most, "the everlasting Light" shone in their town. That expression focuses on Jesus' eternal essence as the divine source of both truth and holiness (cf. Matthew 17:2; 1 John 1:5). Our Lord Himself claimed to be the one divine and eternal Light (John 8:12).

Another definitive title for Jesus is found in the closing line of this hymn: "our Lord Emmanuel." *Emmanuel* literally means "God with us" (Matthew 1:23). It was used more as a title or description than as a proper name. In His incarnation Jesus was, in the most literal sense, God with us.

The Old Testament repeatedly promised that God is present with His people, to secure their destiny in His covenant. The tabernacle was a symbol of that divine presence. The apostle John says Christ became flesh and tabernacled among us (John 1:14). This visible flesh-and-blood incarnation was more intimate and personal than anything most Old Testament believers could have anticipated.

Christ is not only God *with* us, but by faith, the Son of God is *in* us (Colossians 1:27). So this hymn reminds us that "where meek souls will receive him still, the dear Christ enters in." And in the final stanza, the songwriter invites the Savior to "cast out our sin and enter in; be born in us today."

A poet (Angelus Silesius) has written: "Though Christ a thousand times in Bethlehem be born, / But not within thyself, thy soul will be forlorn."

FROM OUT OF THE PAST
Bobbie Wolgemuth

IT WAS A VERY BIG MAN WITH A HEART for little ones who penned the words to this carol. Phillips Brooks was Boston-born, Harvard-educated, and an acclaimed preacher with a dynamic personality. And he loved the people he pastored.

Even though he was sought out by Queen Victoria to preach at the Royal Chapel at Windsor and was offered numerous professorships in prestigious schools, he chose to honor the children in his own church Sunday school above all others. The young people loved their minister too. He was six feet, six inches tall with a personality and a winsome smile to match his stature. He kept a box of toys in his study and encouraged the little ones to visit him. He would stop whatever he was doing and sit and chat with them. It was for these children that he wrote "O Little Town of Bethlehem."

It was close to Christmas when he wrote five eight-line verses about the scene he cherished from a trip to the Holy Land. He was a thirty-year-old bachelor when he took a year-long sabbatical to tour the world. On Christmas Eve he traveled on horseback through the Judean hills where he was told the shepherds saw the angels. Following their path to the Bethlehem Church of the Nativity for an evening service, he was deeply moved. Years later he was able to capture in detail the vivid images of the still night and the silent stars surrounding the manger for the children. He wanted them to hear the angels singing and experience the scene in a new way.

There was no tune for the poem just two days before it was to be sung. So Phillips went to his church organist and Sunday school superintendent, Lewis Redner. He asked Redner to compose a melody the children would like. It was during the night that the inspiration came to Redner, who said he awoke and quickly grabbed a pen to write the complete melody and all the harmony parts that were ringing in his head.

What a Christmas gift for the children, as the organist furiously copied the tune being formed in his mind. How silently, how silently, the wondrous gift *was* given.

Let All Mortal Flesh Keep Silence

LITURGY OF ST. JAMES

FIFTH CENTURY

ADAPTED BY
GERALD MOULTRIE
1864

Let all mortal flesh keep silence, and with fear and trembling stand;
Ponder nothing earthly-minded, for with blessing in his hand,
Christ our God to earth descendeth, our full homage to demand.

King of kings, yet born of Mary, as of old on earth he stood,
Lord of lords, in human vesture, in the body and the blood,
He will give to all the faithful his own self for heav'nly food.

Rank on rank the host of heaven spreads its vanguard on the way,
As the Light of light descendeth from the realms of endless day,
That the pow'rs of hell may vanish as the darkness clears away.

At his feet the six-winged seraph; cherubim, with sleepless eye,
Veil their faces to the presence, as with ceaseless voice they cry,
"Alleluia, alleluia, alleluia, Lord Most High!"

AT THE HEART OF THE HYMN

Joni Eareckson Tada

୭

This is what the Sovereign LORD, the Holy One of Israel, says:
"In repentance and rest is your salvation,
in quietness and trust is your strength,
but you would have none of it."

—ISAIAH 30:15

EVERY YEAR I PRIDE MYSELF ON keeping the month of December on my wall calendar clear. I'll glance up from my desk and admire all those white blocks with nothing written in them. No shopping dates, parties, or appointments. No holiday luncheons or visits from out-of-town friends. I breathe deeply and smile. *This Christmas I'm going to keep the focus on Christ.* Of course, it's only July when I say that.

By the time December 1st rolls around, I am addressing and stamping 350 Christmas cards, ordering the turkey, decorating the house, sending presents back east, checking out sales, buying wrapping paper on discount, rushing back to Rite-Aid for extra tape and ribbon, going to church and office parties, finishing up year-end business, and trying desperately to think of something to give Ken, the husband who has it all.

God always has to tap me on the shoulder. *Joni, remember Me? The reason for the season?* He did that one Christmas when I was sitting by the edge of a Christmas garden set up on the floor of my friend's living room. I was fascinated by the tiny box houses with lights in their windows, the angel-hair snow, and the train.

At the junction of the train station and Main Street, there was a little railroad crossing sign perched by the tracks. I looked closely and read, "Stop . . . look . . . listen."

Stop, I thought, staring at the garden. *Look and listen*. The little bell ding-dinged, and the tiny train clattered along, running in circles. Round and round it traveled, repeating its journey every minute or so. I felt like that train.

God didn't have to tap any harder. *"Be still* before the LORD, all mankind," says Zechariah 2:13. *"Be still*, and know that I am God; I will be exalted among the nations, I will be exalted in the earth," says Psalm 46:10. *"Be still* before the LORD and wait patiently for him," repeats Psalm 37:7.

Stop, look, listen, and be still before the Lord. Good advice. When you discover yourself becoming dulled to the joys of this season, stop. Slow down the pace. Make moments when you look and listen. Take a winter walk. I can't walk, but just the other day I drove the back way home from work and stopped on the crest of a hill to enjoy the early winter sunset while my tape player filled my van with carols. It meant stopping: turning off the engine and putting myself in "park." It meant looking: relishing in the kaleidoscope of pink and lilac, orange and gold smeared across the sunset. It meant listening: thinking about the words to the carols, not just hearing the music.

It meant being still before God. It meant mortal flesh keeping silent. In the quiet and cold, and as stars danced above, I looked out over Malibu Canyon to the darkening, distant mountains and felt as though my heart would break for the loveliness of it all. The loveliness of the Lord's presence.

Shhhh. Stop the chatter and clatter. The God who fills the universe has poured Himself into baby flesh. The high and holy has entered our sinful world. He who shrouds Himself in light, whose chariot is the wind and fire, who crosses the heavens on storm and lightning, who shakes the foundation of the earth . . . He has entered history.

He touched down on this crazy, fragile, and noisy planet. You can hear His Christmas footsteps if you stop, look, listen and . . . be still.

Drop thy still dews of quietness,
Till all our strivings cease;
Take from our souls the strain and stress,
And let our ordered lives confess
The beauty of thy peace.

—JOHN GREENLEAF WHITTIER

IN THE LIGHT OF THE WORD

John MacArthur

IT IS UNIQUE TO BEGIN A HYMN by calling for silence! But this old carol does just that. "Let all mortal flesh keep silence, and with fear and trembling stand; ponder nothing earthly-minded, for with blessing in his hand, Christ our God to earth descendeth, our full homage to demand."

That lofty language calls for the singer to fall quiet with awe and reverence under the power of the reality that the "Lord of lords," "King of kings," "Light of light," "our God," the "Lord Most High" "descendeth from the realms of endless day" and was "born of Mary" as a tiny infant "in human vesture." The reverent praise of heaven is eternally ascribed to Him as seraphim and cherubim "with ceaseless voice . . . cry, 'Alleluia, alleluia, alleluia, Lord Most High!'"

The joy and worship of the angels celebrates two immense accomplishments: the destruction of the "pow'rs of hell" and the salvation of "all the faithful."

The apostle John wrote: "For this purpose the Son of God was manifested, that He might destroy the works of the devil" (1 John 3:8). "The works of the devil" is a comprehensive phrase that includes all of Satan's activities, including temptation, sin, rebellion, deception, persecution, accusation, and even assassination (cf. Luke 8:12; John 8:44; Acts 5:3; 1 Corinthians 7:5; 2 Corinthians 4:4; Ephesians 6:11-12; 1 Thessalonians 2:18; Hebrews 2:14; Revelation 12:10).

The second accomplishment—the salvation of "the faithful"—is expressed in a most provocative and biblical way in the second stanza: "In the body and the blood, he will give to all the faithful his own self for heav'nly food." That truth is drawn from the unforgettable words of Jesus to the Jews:

> *"I am the living bread which came down from heaven. If anyone eats of this*
> *bread, he will live forever; and the bread that I shall give is My flesh."*
>
> —JOHN 6:51

Christ went on to say,

> *"Unless you eat the flesh of the Son of Man and drink His blood, you have no*
> *life in you. Whoever eats My flesh and drinks My blood has eternal life, and I*
> *will raise him up at the last day. For My flesh is food indeed, and My blood is*
> *drink indeed. He who eats My flesh and drinks My blood abides in Me, and I*
> *in him. As the living Father sent Me, and I live because of the Father, so he*
> *who feeds on Me will live because of Me."*
>
> —JOHN 6:53-57

What does this mean? The unbelieving crowd, with their darkened hearts and spiritual deadness, thought Jesus was speaking in literal terms. He did not explain Himself to them, since their minds were willfully darkened and incapable of understanding. But His meaning is clear to those with true faith. He was speaking of the way of salvation. The only way to satisfy one's spiritual hunger and thirst is to swallow—a picturesque way to signify *believing*—to eat and drink the Incarnation and the blood atonement of Jesus Christ.

When sinners are broken, spiritually hungry, and thirsting for righteousness, they will eagerly eat. Jesus is saying that it is not enough to respect Him, to be touched by His unselfish love and tenderness. It is not enough to be sympathetic to His death. The sinner must partake.

And that is what the hymn declares: "In the body and the blood, he will give to all the faithful his own self for heav'nly food." Scripture repeatedly emphasizes that this is the way of salvation. If someone does not believe that God came in human flesh, he cannot be saved (2 John 7).

Nor can anyone be saved without believing in the atoning blood sacrifice of Jesus Christ on the cross (Romans 3:25).

To appropriate the divine, virgin-born, eternal Son of God and embrace with full faith His substitutionary death on the cross is to eat His flesh and blood— an act that gives the life of heaven to the hungry soul.

The hymn thus calls every hungry heart to eat and receive eternal life—and then reverently join the ceaseless praise of the angels ("Rank on rank the host of heaven"), crying, "Alleluia, alleluia, alleluia, Lord Most High!"

FROM OUT OF THE PAST

Dr. Paul Plew

THE FIFTH CENTURY WAS A DESPERATE TIME for the true believer. The medieval church was filled with heresy, selfishness, and the traditions of men.

Those who wanted to worship in spirit and in truth were often persecuted and deprived. To recognize that all creation is only to honor God and not to be earthly-minded was the antithesis of the direction of the leadership of the church.

Saint James's liturgy pattern for public worship was one of the bright lights in the church. It is one of the oldest in the world. It was originally designed for use in the church at Jerusalem. Once it was thought to have been the work of James the Less, half brother of Jesus, but it seems to have taken its earliest form under Cyril of Jerusalem (347 A.D.). The liturgy was written in Greek and modified and expanded for the fifth-century eastern church. It is still used frequently in Eastern Orthodox churches today.

The liturgy actually leads up to the celebration of Communion. It reads: "We remember the sky, the earth and the sea, the sun and the moon, the stars and all creation both rational and irrational, the angels and archangels, powers, mights, dominations, principalities, thrones, the many-eyed Cherubim who also say those words of David: 'Praise the Lord with me.' We remember also the Seraphim, whom Isaias saw in spirit standing around the throne of God, who with two wings cover their faces, with two their feet and with two fly; who say: 'holy, holy, holy, Lord of Sabaoth.' We also say these divine words of the Seraphim, so as to take part in the hymns of the heavenly host."

This helps us understand the hymn that Reverend Moultrie translated in 1864. With his help, we are standing in silenced awe before the cradled King. We contemplate the mystery: He was King of all kings, yet born to an unknown village maiden. Suddenly all the ranks of heaven descend in such intense light that the powers of darkness flee in terror before them. And the angels cover their faces because of the brilliance of the light of heaven. They cry in ceaseless voices, "Alleluia, alleluia, alleluia."

Let's not pattern our Advent season after thunderous celebrations and meaningless festivities, but spend sufficient time contemplating Him in reverential worship and silenced wonder.

Silent Night! Holy Night!

JOSEPH MOHR

1792-1848

Silent night! Holy night! All is calm, all is bright
Round yon virgin mother and child.
Holy infant, so tender and mild,
Sleep in heavenly peace, sleep in heavenly peace.

Silent night! Holy night! Shepherds quake at the sight!
Glories stream from heaven afar,
Heav'nly hosts sing alleluia;
Christ, the Savior, is born! Christ, the Savior, is born!

Silent night! Holy night! Son of God, love's pure light
Radiant beams from thy holy face,
With the dawn of redeeming grace,
Jesus, Lord, at thy birth, Jesus, Lord, at thy birth.

Silent night! Holy night! Wondrous star, lend thy light;
With the angels let us sing
Alleluia to our King;
Christ, the Savior, is born! Christ, the Savior, is born!

At the Heart of the Hymn

Robert Wolgemuth

❧

Then a great and powerful wind tore the mountains apart and shattered the rocks
*before the L*ORD*, but the L*ORD *was not in the wind . . . the earthquake . . . the*
fire. And after the fire came a gentle whisper.

—1 KINGS 19:11-12

*I*MISSED OUT ON a lot at Christmas.

On Christmas Eve, we were in church. My neighborhood buddies were home
with their families, watching TV or ripping open presents. But not my family.
We were sitting quietly in a worship service with a bunch of grownups, singing
carols like "Silent Night." "Silent" night? You can say that again.

The next morning, in the predawn darkness, when my friends were still asleep,
I had *Chicago Tribunes* to deliver. No more nestling in a warm bed and no danc-
ing sugar plums for me. Only heavy newspapers, slippery streets, and bitter
cold to welcome Christmas Day. It hadn't only been a silent night—it was a
pretty silent morning, too.

Once back home, while the presents sat undisturbed under the tree, there
was a hot shower and a healthy family breakfast.

Finally, once the kitchen had been cleaned up and the dishes washed and put
away, it was time for opening presents. But did we collectively get to dive in and
shred the wrapping on the gifts that were ours? Not a chance. Instead my dad
would start singing "Joy to the World," his all-time favorite hymn. We'd join in.
Then our parents made us all sit quietly and listen to the reading of the Christmas
story. Like we've never heard *this* before? Then my dad would offer a prayer of
thanksgiving for God's bountiful goodness. And, speaking of thanks, he'd never

make this prayer too long. It was mercifully crisp and to the point. The anxious shifting of his six children let him know that their patience was razor-thin.

Now can we tear into the stuff? we'd all be thinking. No, order must still prevail. My younger brother and sister, the twins, were responsible to pass out the gifts . . . one at a time. And we all had to sit still and watch each present being ceremoniously opened. "Be careful. Let's see if we can use that beautiful wrapping paper again." And once the gift inside had been exposed, the recipient would say "thank you" to the giver. Really *good* stuff warranted a hug.

Truthfully, most of the gifts were practical things. Because of my paper route, I usually got a new pair of warm gloves or a wool scarf. Necessary school supplies were also quite popular. I remember my brother getting a hand-held calculator. Two hugs for that. Very few "gifty" things . . . almost *never* something excessive or frivolous. Although I *do* remember my first bottle of cologne.

Round and round the circle we'd go until the tree stood naked in the corner of the room, with no wrapped boxes to cover its feet.

Wait, one more tradition. We got to pray one more time to "thank the Lord for His goodness and for family and for the joy of giving and receiving. Amen."

Now do you understand why I thought I missed out on so much? Our Christmas Eve had been spent in quiet worship, singing, and praising the birth of the infant King. And our Christmas morning had been so ordered, so thoughtfully executed, so honoring of the Savior, so respectful of each other, so . . . German.

Wait until I have a family of my own, I'd think to myself. *We're going to go crazy at Christmas. Forget all this tradition. It'll be every man for himself.*

We spent last Christmas with our children and grandchildren. Their Christmas Eve and their Christmas morning looked almost *exactly* like my parents' Christmas had. I wonder where *that* tradition came from? Worshipful, breakfast together, an honoring of Jesus, and one-gift-at-a-time respect for each other, just like *my* parents' Christmas.

Radiant beams from thy holy face,

With the dawn of redeeming grace,

Jesus, Lord at thy birth,

Jesus, Lord at thy birth.

My family has taught me to cherish the wonder of this silent and holy night with tenderness and respect. What a priceless gift.

IN THE LIGHT OF THE WORD
John MacArthur

THE NIGHT OF CHRIST'S BIRTH may have actually been anything but tranquil in a noisy stable in an overcrowded town. But the first verse of this hymn presents a picture of serenity, reflecting the state in which the shepherds found Christ, "wrapped in swaddling cloths, lying in a manger" (Luke 2:12). It was an inauspicious beginning for the incarnate Lord of all, but the surprising quietness with which He came to earth is the whole focus of this beloved hymn.

Stanza 2 further sets the scene by recalling the biblical account of the shepherds, their fear of the angels, and the glory streaming down from heaven and shining all around them (Luke 2:8-9).

The heart of the hymn is the third stanza. There the Holy Infant is introduced as "Son of God, love's pure light" bearing "radiant beams from [His] holy face." Then comes the high point of the lyrics—and the whole purpose of the birth of the Savior. He is bringing "the dawn of redeeming grace." His arrival meant the end of the long night of darkness, and the dawning of the long-promised redemption.

Redemption is the central theme of virtually all the biblical promises about the coming Messiah. Before His birth, the angel of the Lord had appeared to Joseph and said,

> *[Mary] will bring forth a Son, and you shall call His name JESUS, for He will save His people from their sins.*
>
> —MATTHEW 1:21

Even His name signified "the dawn of redeeming grace." That name means, "Jehovah saves." He was coming "to seek and to save that which was lost" (Luke 19:10). Mary understood this perfectly, as is clear from her song of praise—the Magnificat—in Luke 1:46-55.

We can only imagine the overwhelming emotions that must have churned in Mary as she realized her womb contained the Savior of the world. On one hand, the privilege of being the mother of Messiah had no doubt been a cherished hope of Jewish girls for generations. Mary knew she was uniquely blessed, and many generations would affirm her so.

On the other hand, she was in a difficult situation as a young girl. She would have to face the stigma of unwed motherhood. There would be disgrace heaped on her from some who didn't know the truth, and she could be an outcast to people who did not believe her story. And why should they? She was only the simple wife-to-be of a carpenter, who himself was no one special—a maker of yokes, plows, and wooden furnishings.

Scripture tells us repeatedly that "Mary kept all these things and pondered them in her heart" (Luke 2:19; cf. v. 51). Her silence on that holy, "silent night" masked the profound thoughts that filled her heart.

It's vital to remember that Christmas represents only "the *dawn* of redeeming grace," and not the complete fullness of it. In order for Christ to provide salvation for sinners, He had to live a life of perfect obedience to the law, and then die to pay the price of sin on others' behalf.

Sometimes at Christmas we get so swept up in celebrating the Babe in the manger that we forget this is merely the beginning of the redemptive story. Christ's birth is not what redeems us from sin; His death is.

> *Without shedding of blood there is no remission [of sins].*
> —HEBREWS 9:22
> *It is the blood that makes atonement for the soul.*
> —LEVITICUS 17:11

Therefore when the angel told Joseph that Christ was coming to save His people from their sins, he was in effect saying that Christ was coming to die. This fact is not often stressed at Christmas, but it is the very heart of the true Christmas story. Jesus Himself said, "The Son of Man . . . [came] to give His life a ransom for many" (Matthew 20:28).

Jesus also said, "I lay down My life for the sheep" (John 10:15).

So the next time you contemplate the events of that silent, holy night, remember that the Babe in the manger is coming to earth with the express purpose of dying. And then with Mary and "with the angels let us sing alleluia to our King; Christ, the Savior, is born! Christ, the Savior, is born!"

FROM OUT OF THE PAST
Bobbie Wolgemuth

THERE IS A TENDER YEARNING FOR father and family that surrounds the poem written by pastor Joseph Mohr. He was born to a poor unwed woman named Anna Schoiber in a small Austrian village. Her lover, and the father of her baby, deserted her before Joseph's birth and joined the army as a musketeer. Moving into a small room with her mother where she knitted to make a living, Anna was forced to provide for herself and the baby.

Even though destitute, she made sure Joseph was baptized just hours after his birth and appointed a local villager to be his godfather. Anna wanted young Joseph to receive a proper education and made sure he grew up under the tutelage of the church. The cathedral choirmaster became a foster father to Joseph, who loved singing. Even as a boy, his talent was recognized as he sang in the St. Peter's choir directed by none other than the great composer Michael Haydn.

Joseph continued to receive honors for his work even in grammar school and went on to complete a seminary degree in Salzburg before he was ordained as a priest at age twenty-three.

It was in a small village church, where he was assistant pastor at twenty-six, that Joseph wanted a Christmas song that he could play on his much-loved guitar. As he was planning a special service for the December 24th evening vespers, he showed the six-verse poem he had written to his church organist and choir director, Franz Gruber. Joseph later told a group of young seminarians that one of the most precious moments of his life was when he spoke to his comrade, Gruber, about a joint writing effort. He said, "The two of us did something for the Holy Night. I transcribed the words and Franz the melody."

Little did the two friends know that their carol would become the most widely translated Christmas song in history, as well as the most popular.

Although we no longer sing them, the original German words give us insight into the heart of the young man who wrote the text. The references to family and father show us the unfulfilled childhood longings he still held as a grown man. Verse 1, translated from the original, said, "Round yon godly tender pair, holy infant with curly hair."

There were frequent references to God as Father throughout the extended text. In the fifth verse Mohr reveals his own thankfulness for his heavenly Father who brought redemption to the darkness of history.

Long ago, minding our plight,
God the world from misery freed,
In the dark age of our fathers decreed,
All the world redeemed. All the world redeemed.

As cozy pictures of hearth and home swept through his childhood longings, Joseph Mohr found his Father's arms a comfortable place to rest. From that place he gave the world a Christmas carol that still wraps us in heavenly peace today.

Hark!
the Herald
Angels
Sing

CHARLES WESLEY

1707-1788

Hark! the herald angels sing, "Glory to the newborn King;
Peace on earth, and mercy mild, God and sinners reconciled!"
Joyful, all ye nations, rise, join the triumph of the skies;
With th' angelic host proclaim, "Christ is born in Bethlehem!"
Hark! the herald angels sing, "Glory to the newborn King."

Christ, by highest heav'n adored, Christ, the everlasting Lord!
Late in time behold him come, offspring of the Virgin's womb.
Veiled in flesh the Godhead see; hail th' incarnate Deity,
Pleased as man with men to dwell, Jesus, our Emmanuel.
Hark! the herald angels sing, "Glory to the newborn King."

Hail the heav'n-born Prince of Peace! Hail the Sun of Righteousness!
Light and life to all he brings, ris'n with healing in his wings.
Mild he lays his glory by, born that man no more may die,
Born to raise the sons of earth, born to give them second birth.
Hark! the herald angels sing, "Glory to the newborn King."

At the Heart of the Hymn

Robert Wolgemuth

ꭣ

Be strong in the Lord and in his mighty power. Put on the full armor of God so that you can take your stand against the devil's schemes.

—EPHESIANS 6:10-11

MY WIFE, BOBBIE, IS AN ANGEL COLLECTOR. Take a quick walk through our house and you'll know what I mean. We have porcelain angels, crystal angels, angels embroidered on pillows, books about angels, angel candlesticks and coasters . . . we even have a few angel teddy bears.

But as hard as you look, you'll not find a single angel like the ones this Christmas carol describes. These angels—the herald angels—would be more appropriately dressed in army fatigues than white linen and lace. We are witnessing a full military exercise, not a few little kids skipping around on a stage with fluffy robes, coat-hanger wings, and tilting halos.

Herald angels—a perfect symbol of might and power. Even today in Great Britain, Scottish heralds are the supreme officers of honor and counsel to the sovereign in all military matters. The herald is the head of the whole executive department of the law.

These were more than simply angelic messengers that Christmas night. These angels meant business. Their announcement of "peace on earth" was not simply a pleasant greeting to a humble group of sheep herders. Their words meant that this event would mark the end of the greatest war in history—"God and sinners reconciled." The Holy One of Israel was sitting at the same table with us, His sinful adversaries. This was the final negotiation of an eternal armistice.

On November 9, 1989, the great wall that split Germany in two came down.

For twenty-eight years, the Berlin Wall had been the symbol of freedom versus socialist bondage, of hope versus despair. But on this day the wall Winston Churchill dubbed as part of the "Iron Curtain" came down. Since 1961 over 100 people had perished trying to scale it. But no more. Stoic Germans from one side shamelessly wept as they embraced their estranged loved ones from the other side.

Germany was once again one nation . . . one people.

But how did this happen? What was it that ended almost three decades of separation? Was it a kindly handshake and a diplomatic smile? Or was it something else?

Two years before the wall came down, President Ronald Reagan walked to a podium in West Berlin. "Mr. Gorbachev," he boldly commanded the Prime Minister of the Soviet Union, "open this gate! Mr. Gorbachev, tear down this wall!"

Diplomats around the world sucked in a collective gasp. How could he be so bold? But President Reagan was not to be denied. His confidence came from the unprecedented strength of America's military and his unswerving belief in the immorality of communism. Two years later, bowing under the pressure of sheer intimidation, Mikhail Gorbachev tore down the wall and set a nation free.

The herald angels had a message for humanity that Christmas night. The Peacemaker had come. The Sovereign God of the universe was visiting earth, and the great wall separating the perfect Creator from His sinful creation was coming down.

"Hail the heav'n-born Prince of Peace," the herald shouted, standing at military readiness. "Hail the Sun of Righteousness."

Oh, how the Prince of Darkness must have cowered on the night we were set free.

IN THE LIGHT OF THE WORD

John MacArthur

HIS FAMILIAR HYMN IS RICH with a treasury of titles for Jesus: "King," "Christ," "everlasting Lord," "Sun of Righteousness," "Prince of Peace," "Emmanuel." His heavenly glory is also celebrated: He is "heav'n-born," "the Godhead see[n]," "incarnate Deity." His earthly humiliation is told in the following words: He is "born," "offspring of the Virgin's womb," and "veiled in flesh," He "lays his glory by." The blessings of His coming are given in many facets: "peace," "mercy," "light," "life," "healing," "second birth," and resurrection to eternal joy.

But one phrase stands out among all the titles and biblical expressions of this hymn, summing up the whole reason for the Incarnation. This is *why* the saints and angels sing: "God and sinners reconciled." That was the work He came to accomplish.

That thought drives us to Paul's letter to the church in Corinth:

> *Now all things are of God, who has reconciled us to Himself through Jesus Christ, and has given us the ministry of reconciliation, that is, that God was in Christ reconciling the world to Himself, not imputing their trespasses to them, and has committed to us the word of reconciliation. Now then, we are ambassadors for Christ, as though God were pleading through us: We implore you on Christ's behalf, be reconciled to God.*
> —2 CORINTHIANS 5:18-20

This is the greatest of all truths for the sinner—reconciliation with God! Five times in those verses in 2 Corinthians some form of the word *reconciliation* is used. God Himself seeks to be reconciled to sinners. No aspect of the Christmas message is more important than that one.

Such reconciliation once seemed impossible. Scripture teaches that our holy God is alienated and estranged from sinners. He is angry with the wicked every day (Psalm 7:11). He has justly determined that all are worthy of eternal punishment.

From that standpoint, the enmity appeared hopeless. A perfectly holy God whose justice must be satisfied by punishing sinners would seem the sovereign Enemy of a helpless, fallen race. The divine hostility appeared irreversible. And from man's side it is. None of us could ever please Him so as to change our own condition.

But happily, from God's side, the situation is not hopeless! God, in His infinite mercy and grace, has determined for His own glory to provide reconciliation to sinners.

How can God offer reconciliation to sinners and still be just? To borrow language from Romans 4:5, how can He be just and the justifier of the ungodly? How can He dismiss the guilt of the sinner?

The answer is in 2 Corinthians 5:21:

> *He made Him who knew no sin to be sin for us, that we might become the righteousness of God in Him.*

In other words, God put His own beloved Son in the sinner's place and punished Him. Peter wrote:

> *[Christ] Himself bore our sins in His own body on the tree, that we, having died to sins, might live for righteousness.*
>
> —1 PETER 2:24

It is for that very reason that "Christ [was] born in Bethlehem." He came to provide the way of reconciliation. God sacrificed His own Son in order to purchase reconciliation for sinners.

There is no more powerful truth in Scripture! It is the very heart of the gospel message. And that is why I consider it the most potent line in Wesley's great hymn—"God and sinners reconciled."

Every believer partakes in "the ministry of reconciliation." In other words, it is our privilege to proclaim the same message originally heralded by the angels. God "has committed to us the word of reconciliation." So our most important ministry as believers is to tell sinners how they may be reconciled to God. Spreading that message is the church's chief purpose on earth. We echo the news brought by angels in this most wonderful of all truths. This *is* the good news of Christmas.

So, for God's amazing reconciliation with us we join the angels in giving "glory to the newborn King."

FROM OUT OF THE PAST

Bobbie Wolgemuth

IT WAS THE PASSION OF CHARLES WESLEY to move people—young and old, rich and poor, wise and simple—to real faith by singing words of theology and devotion. His education in doctrine and prose began at home where he was taught to memorize Scripture and sing psalms every morning before breakfast. Charles continued his education at Oxford University, where he and his brother John met with an accountability group of serious-minded students who called themselves The Holy Club. Besides discussing deep theological issues and social concerns, the young men confessed their sins and prayed for one another. They made a covenant "that none of us will undertake anything of importance without first proposing it to the others" and that if there were disagreements they would "beg God's direction" before deciding by lot. These friends experienced ministry together, preached in the streets of England, and organized mission work both in Europe and abroad.

Fearing that "heart religion" was dying in the Anglican Church, Charles and his brother John organized bands of small groups kindled by singing, fellowship, and faith sharing. Charles wrote hymns and directions for their singing, saying, "I design plain truth for plain people. We ought not to discourage believers from rejoicing evermore. Let them rejoice unto God, with reverence, always happy in God!"

The Anglican Church was trying to subdue all but the most liturgical forms of music for worship. But many of the townspeople were beginning to warm up to these new poetic words, set to folk tunes and ballads by the Reformers. Being accused of singing words set to the "devil's music," John and Charles instructed their followers to "Beware of singing as if you were half dead, or half asleep; but lift up your voice with strength. Be no more afraid of your voice now, nor more ashamed of its being heard than when you sung the songs of Satan."

This carol is one of the two Advent hymns authorized to be sung in the Anglican Church. It was written by Charles and was called "A Hymn for Christmas Day." The original ten stanzas began with a popular English phrase, "the sky rings," describing the angelic announcement as being so loud that all the firmament was vaulted in an arch of heavenly noise. Later translations shortened the hymn and changed "the sky rings" to "herald angels."

The tune that carries "Hark, the Herald Angels Sing" was written by the great composer, conductor, and performer Felix Mendelssohn, celebrating the anniversary of the invention of printing. Knowing it would be a piece very much liked by both singers and hearers, he had it sent to music editors to find a suitable poem for it. His only instructions were for the editors to try to find a national and merry subject, something that would fit the happy, popular tune. He added, "It will never do to sacred words." Little did he know that Charles Wesley had written a condensed course in biblical doctrine in poetic form that was in search of a melody. The marriage of the verse to Mendelssohn's tune was one of God's great surprises for our hymnbooks. Still today, it's one Christmas song where we can follow Charles's directions to "sing lustily with good courage and see that the heart is offered to God continually."

Lo, How a Rose E'er Blooming

THEODORE BAKER
1851-1934

HARRIET SPAETH
1845-1925

VERSE 5 TRANSLATED BY
JOHN C. MATTES
IN 1914

Lo, how a rose e'er blooming from tender stem hath sprung,
Of Jesse's lineage coming, as men of old have sung.
It came, a flow'ret bright, amid the cold of winter,
when half-spent was the night.

Isaiah 'twas foretold it, the rose I have in mind;
with Mary we behold it, the virgin mother kind.
To show God's love aright she bore to men a Savior,
when half-spent was the night.

The shepherds heard the story, proclaimed by angels bright,
How Christ, the Lord of glory, was born on earth this night.
To Bethlehem they sped and in the manger found him,
as angel heralds said.

This flow'r whose fragrance tender with sweetness fills the air,
Dispels with glorious splendor the darkness ev'rywhere.
True man, yet very God; from sin and death he saves us
and lightens ev'ry load.

O Savior, child of Mary, who felt our human woe;
O Savior, King of glory, who dost our weakness know,
Bring us at length, we pray, to the bright courts of heaven
and to the endless day.

AT THE HEART OF THE HYMN

Joni Eareckson Tada

ੑ

A shoot will come up from the stump of Jesse;

from his roots a Branch will bear fruit.

—ISAIAH 11:1

EVERY FAMILY HAS ITS CHRISTMAS TRADITIONS, and Ken and I are no exception. For us, it's dressing in our finest and treating the rest of the family to a fabulous holiday dinner at Lawry's Prime Rib in Beverly Hills. We drive slowly down Wilshire Boulevard, oohing and ahhing at the store window displays, the decorations crowning each intersection, the lampposts trimmed with poinsettias, and the Beverly Wilshire Hotel with its huge Christmas tree out front. With "Silver Bells" echoing down the boulevard, the only thing that's missing is snow.

Lawry's Prime Rib is an elegant restaurant. Valet parking with guys in tuxedos. A grand entrance that opens into a warm and beautifully decorated salon. And best of all, the finest prime rib west of Kansas City. Crystal and linen, silver and candlelight. Even a carver in his tall chef's hat, pushing his cart loaded with racks of ribs so he can slice the exact cut you want. I get a charge out of Ken when he beams, "I'll take the Diamond Jim Brady end cut, please! The part with all the pepper and spices." (As if the carver needed a reminder.)

While dining, it's fun watching the carolers go from table to table singing everyone's favorite Christmas carol. They're dressed Victorian style, like a quartet straight out of a Charles Dickens novel, all in capes, ladies in fur-trimmed hats, and the bass singer holding a staff decorated with a holly wreath and bells. I keep an eye on them, waiting for them to walk down our aisle.

"Let me guess," says Ken between bites. "You're going to ask them to sing 'Lo, How a Rose E'er Blooming.'" "Yes," I say, "and I might even do the alto part."

It's tradition.

When the carolers stop by our table and I ask them to sing this, my favorite Christmas hymn, they look surprised. No one ever requests "Lo, How a Rose E'er Blooming." Sometimes one of them will recognize me as the lady who "always picks this one!" But no one complains. The quartet loves this carol too. The harmony is mystifying and deeply moving.

Lo, how a rose e'er blooming from tender stem hath sprung,
Of Jesse's lineage coming, as men of old have sung.
It came, a flow'ret bright, amid the cold of winter,
when half-spent was the night.

One more thing about the tradition: We carry Kleenex. This hymn always makes me cry. There's something about the way the song intertwines—the melody part weaving in and out of the other parts—that transports me to a monastery from another century, listening to an ancient madrigal, so beautiful and seductive in its sweetness.

By the time the carolers conclude the last note, I'm coming out of a dream. To me, this song has always been an invitation to see and feel, to know and experience *more* of what Christmas really means. It pulls mysteriously on our hearts, bidding us to go beyond, to "step into the other side" of Christmas. It is an inkling, a hint, a whisper of an even greater celebration yet to happen. On this side of eternity, Christmas is still a promise. Yes, the Savior has come, but the story is not finished. There is peace in our hearts . . . but we long for peace in our world.

Soon and very soon the Rose of Sharon will return and, with Him, all the fragrance and joy of a longing fulfilled. Until then, we sing the last verse:

O Savior, child of Mary, who felt our human woe;
O Savior, King of glory, who dost our weakness know,
Bring us at length, we pray, to the bright courts
of heaven and to the endless day.

IN THE LIGHT OF THE WORD

John MacArthur

THIS ANCIENT CAROL PICTURES CHRIST metaphorically as a rose. The imagery is based on Isaiah 11:1: "Then a shoot will spring from the stem of Jesse, and a branch from his roots will bear fruit" (NASB). The hymn-writer envisions the fruit of the branch as a beautiful flower—a rose.

The biblical reference is made clear at the outset of the second stanza: "Isaiah 'twas foretold it, the rose I have in mind." He also mentions "Jesse's lineage," further identifying the scriptural source of his metaphor.

The poetic language pictures a frail "flow'ret," "blooming from tender stem" in the most unexpected circumstances—"amid the cold of winter, when half-spent was the night."

The meaning of the metaphor is made explicit with the mention of Mary, "the virgin mother kind." The frail rose is the infant Christ. The familiar features of the biblical account are mentioned too—"the shepherds," the "angels," and "Bethlehem."

The nature of Christ is clearly presented in the hymn: "True man, yet very God," "King of glory," and "Savior." And His saving work is described in the fourth stanza: "From sin and death he saves us and lightens ev'ry load."

One magnificent truth concerning Christ, not found in most carols, is featured in the fifth stanza: "O Savior, King of glory, who dost our weakness know, bring us at length, we pray, to the bright courts of heaven and to the endless day." That describes the wondrous ministry of the Savior as our faithful High Priest. It is an allusion to Hebrews 2:17:

> In all things He had to be made like His brethren, that He might be a merciful and faithful High Priest in things pertaining to God, to make propitiation for the sins of the people.

He knows our weakness because He "was in all points tempted as we are, yet without sin" (Hebrews 4:15).

He is the perfect Mediator. As no other go-between could, He represents God before His people and His people before God. He erases the fear that God is far removed from human life and concerns. He has fully experienced our feelings, our emotions, our temptations, and our pain. In fact, He became man to triumph over the temptation and suffering that plague us.

He is therefore a sympathetic and understanding High Priest. He has been through every kind of human trial Himself. He experienced hunger and thirst and exhaustion. He was tempted by Satan personally. At the tomb of Lazarus He shed tears of grief. In the Garden of Gethsemane, just before His arrest, His sweat was like great drops of blood. Those were real, human agonies He suffered. He knows our pain and sorrow.

And this same High Priest, who experienced every ordeal of human life and death, is now at the right hand of the Father interceding for us (Hebrews 7:25).

He understands us perfectly and therefore "is also able to save to the uttermost those who come to God through Him."

And so by Christ's sacrifice of Himself, God's throne of judgment is turned into a throne of grace for those who trust in Him.

The Bible speaks much of God's justice. But how terrible for us if He were only just and not also gracious! Sinful people *deserve* death. That is the sentence of justice. But we *need* salvation, and that is a gift of grace. Here is a sympathetic High Priest who "did not come to destroy men's lives but to save them" (Luke 9:56). He has turned the heavenly seat of divine justice into a throne of mercy.

How can anyone reject such a High Priest, such a Savior—who not only permits us to come before His throne for grace and help, but pleads with us to come in confidence (Hebrews 4:16)? Come, receive grace and mercy when you need it—before it is too late and your heart is hard and God's "today" is over (Hebrews 3:15; 2 Corinthians 6:2). The day of salvation is now.

Those who trust Him can be certain this faithful High Priest, who intercedes for them, will "bring us at length . . . to the bright courts of heaven and to the endless day."

FROM OUT OF THE PAST
Bobbie Wolgemuth

OVER THE CENTURIES THE ROMAN CHURCH had created a wall dividing God and man. In Germany, before the Reformers could bring all the Bible to all the people in their own tongue, the Word was hidden in liturgies only the clergy and schooled young men could understand. It was from Germany, in the mid-sixteenth century, that the Reformers passionately called for a service in which "the Order is for the simple and for the young folk. They must daily be exercised in the Scripture and God's Word to the end that they may become conversant with Scripture and expert in its use, ready and skilful in giving an answer for their faith, and able in time to teach others."

Men like Martin Luther and the German Reformers thought that the hymn singing should be for everyone, not just the few in the choir loft. In a proposal to the Church in 1526, Luther pled, "We must read, sing, preach, write, and compose; and if it could in any wise help or promote their interests, I would have all the bells pealing, and all the organs playing, and everything making a noise that could."

It was against this backdrop that clergymen and skilled editors adapted church creeds and various prayers and liturgies into a popular and memorable musical form.

At the same time that carols were written to warm the cold chill of the cathedrals, the paintings of great masters all over Europe were rich with images of the Nativity. Winter snow often adorned the manger scene. Nativity scenes frequently included genteel portraits of mothers and children. The use of a rose tree in these settings—identifying Jesus as the Rose of Sharon—was also common.

No longer was sound theology locked up in mysterious Latin phrases. It now could be seen and heard and experienced by all the people. Combining art images, biblical passages, and music would bind the lesson like a corded rope to impress the truth of Scripture on German parishioners.

The English translator of stanzas 1 and 2, Theodore Baker, lived in Germany and was a noted researcher and music editor. He translated another favorite into English, "We Gather Together." Baker wrote a reference book for serious music scholars entitled *Biographical Dictionary of Musicians*. He found in his research a collection of verse originally used in a Catholic book entitled *Father Conrad's Little Prayer Book*. The nineteen-stanza prayer was shortened and adapted to the haunting melody of "Lo! How a Rose E'er Blooming." Harriet Spaeth translated verses 3 and 4 and John Mattes verse 5 to give us a poetic rendering of Christian creed, Old Testament prophecy, and music to celebrate a wintry nativity.

Angels from the Realms of Glory

JAMES MONTGOMERY

1771-1854

Angels, from the realms of glory, wing your flight o'er all the earth;
Ye who sang creation's story, now proclaim Messiah's birth:
Come and worship, come and worship, worship Christ,
the newborn King.

Shepherds in the fields abiding, watching o'er your flocks by night,
God with man is now residing, yonder shines the infant Light:
Come and worship, come and worship, worship Christ,
the newborn King.

Sages, leave your contemplations, brighter visions beam afar;
Seek the great Desire of nations; ye have seen his natal star:
Come and worship, come and worship, worship Christ,
the newborn King.

Saints before the altar bending, watching long in hope and fear,
Suddenly the Lord, descending, in his temple shall appear:
Come and worship, come and worship, worship Christ,
the newborn King.

All creation, join in praising God the Father, Spirit, Son;
Evermore your voices raising to th' eternal Three in One:
Come and worship, come and worship, worship Christ,
the newborn King.

At the Heart of the Hymn
Robert Wolgemuth

൦

Come, all you who are thirsty . . . come, buy and eat!
Why spend money on what is not bread,
And your labor on what does not satisfy? . . .
Give ear and come to me; hear me, that your soul may live.

—Isaiah 55:1-3

Come and get it!" Wild-West moms hollered from the back door, the sound of their voices almost drowned out by the clanging on the large triangle that hung there.

"Come and get it!"

Although we didn't get our own television until I was in the sixth grade, I can remember watching shows at my friends' houses. The TV of choice was the one at David Engeseth's, because he had a remote . . . a clicker. As youngsters, changing the channels without moving from the sofa was such magic.

I loved the westerns: *Gunsmoke*, *Bonanza*, *The Rifleman*. My heroes were tough. They were so sure of themselves and always creamed the bad guys. Plus there was something magnetic about living in the wide-open spaces, owning horses, and not having to bathe every day. Boys. How did our mothers survive?

When it was mealtime in the Old West, moms—or in the case of the Ponderosa, Hop Sing the Cook—would open the back door and bang on the huge steel triangle. The words "Come and get it!" brought hungry family members and ranch hands running for a hearty meal. Breakfast, lunch, or dinner, these hard-working folks knew there would be plenty for everyone to eat. And unlike some of the mothers in our neighborhood who had to call more than once to get their kids in for a meal, the first sounds of the clanging triangle always brought every-one right away.

"Come and worship," this Christmas hymn calls. "Come and worship." It even says it twice. "Worship Christ, the newborn King."

I love the image of the angels, the shepherds, the sages, the saints, and all creation rushing to the manger at the sound of the invitation. Hungry people looking for the Bread of Life. Thirsty folks longing for Living Water . . . all hud-dled at the manger cradling the Savior who satisfies.

Although I'm only a layman, church building projects have seemed to follow me around. When we lived in Texas, our church underwent a massive capital campaign to expand the property. Less than a year after we moved to Nashville, our new church did the same. Just before we left Nashville to move to central Florida, that same church was about to launch another effort in brick and mor-tar. And six months after we moved to Central Florida . . . you guessed it, another church building project.

I've had various minor responsibilities in these efforts, but looking back, I wish I had done something more—I wish I had encouraged hanging a massive trian-gle by one of the back doors of the church.

When it came time for Advent, I would have suggested to the Sunday school superintendent that every class should take a short field trip to the triangle. The teachers could have told their own version of mealtime in the Wild West and then had the children try their hand at clanging and singing, "Come and worship, come and worship, worship Christ, the newborn King."

Worship is not simply a gathering of folks on weekends, paying God a pleas-ant visit with a song and a sermon. Worship is life to hungry people who feel like they would die without it. It brings them into the presence of the King who satisfies.

Run. Don't walk. "Come and get it!"

IN THE LIGHT OF THE WORD
John MacArthur

℘

*T*HE FLOW OF THIS HYMN sweeps through the New Testament, beginning with the account of the Gospels and ending with the book of Revelation. The opening word in each of the first four stanzas singles out a specific group for praise of the Messiah's birth:

Stanza 1—"angels"
Stanza 2—"shepherds"
Stanza 3—"sages"
Stanza 4—"saints"
Stanza 5—"all creation"

There is a chronological sequence in those groups: The "angels" and "shepherds" were there on the night of His birth (Luke 2:8-14). The "sages," the wise men, came later, finding Him not in a stable or a manger, but in a house (Matthew 2:11). "Saints" includes all believers of this age. And at the consummation of human history, all of redeemed creation in glory will unite in never-ceasing praise to the Trinity.

The short refrain repeatedly calls all to "worship Christ, the newborn King." So the song is all about worship, especially stressing the fact that Christ is worthy to be worshiped by all creatures without exception.

The first stanza focuses on the worship of the angels, and it links the worship of the angels at creation with their worship at the birth of Christ ("Ye who sang creation's story, now proclaim Messiah's birth"). The singing of creation's story is no doubt a reference to Job 38:7, where we learn that at creation, "the morning stars sang together, and all the sons of God shouted for joy." (The expression "sons of God" signifies angels throughout the book of Job—cf. Job 1:6; 2:1.)

The birth of Christ was an event the significance of which was unparalleled by anything since the creation of the universe. So it was fitting that the angels celebrated His birth with an outpouring of praise such as had not been seen since the dawn of creation.

The glorious praise offered at Christ's birth by "a multitude of the heavenly host" (Luke 2:13) contrasts starkly with the meager worship offered by a handful of lowly shepherds. Christ's birth, as momentous as it was, went largely unnoticed by humanity.

Even among the people of God, where expectation of the Messiah was running high, almost no one noticed His coming. Their expectations were all wrong. They were looking for a conquering hero, not an "infant Light." And if the host of angels had not specifically revealed His whereabouts to those shepherds, it appears that the only human worshipers at the manger would have been Joseph and Mary.

And yet, as the third stanza of this song reminds us, the wider world was not left without a witness. God sovereignly drew sages from far away to "come and worship." Wise men from the east, drawn to Him by His "natal star," found "the great Desire of nations" and gave Him gifts befitting a king. The expression "Desire of nations" is a reference to Haggai 2:7, one of several Old Testament messianic promises that predicted Israel's Messiah would have a ministry that extended to the Gentiles. The coming of the wise men was also a fulfillment of Isaiah 65:1:

> I was sought by those who did not ask for Me; I was found by those who did not seek Me. I said, "Here I am, here I am," to a nation that was not called by My name.
>
> —quoted in Romans 10:20

Although so few noticed His birth, the chorus of praise has swelled over the years as multitudes have found Him—or rather been found and redeemed by Him. And the fourth stanza celebrates that fact. It evokes the image of "saints before the altar bending"—a reference especially reminiscent of the martyrs described in Revelation 6:9, "who [have] been slain for the word of God and for the testimony which they held."

The final stanza speaks of the praise that will redound throughout eternity in heaven, also described in the closing book of Scripture:

> *And every creature which is in heaven and on the earth and under the earth and such as are in the sea, and all that are in them, I heard saying: "Blessing and honor and glory and power be to Him who sits on the throne, and to the Lamb, forever and ever!"*
>
> *—Revelation 5:13*

FROM OUT OF THE PAST

Bobbie Wolgemuth

TRUE GENIUS OFTEN GOES unrecognized or unappreciated until many years later. Such is the case of the gift of Scottish-born James Montgomery.

Montgomery was dismissed from an English Moravian seminary for his obsession with poetry when he was only in his twenties. This, coupled with the news of the death of both his parents who were missionaries in the West Indies, could have completely devastated young James. But it didn't.

Drawing on what his parents had taught him from Scripture and a genuine concern for others that they had instilled in him, James was energized to use his pen to champion the cause of the weak, including those caught in slavery. As a newspaperman, he quickly became editor of the *Sheffield Register* in London, but he suffered at the hands of those who disagreed with what he wrote.

He was put in prison twice for his controversial ideas—once for printing a song supporting the storming of the Bastille in the French Revolution and once for "biased reporting" of a reform riot in Sheffield. Even while behind bars, he continued writing controversial and persuasive poetry to champion the downtrodden. When he was just twenty-six, he published a volume of poems called *Prison Amusements*, which included verse from those dark days of imprisonment.

It was Christmas Eve, twenty years later, when the rich imagery and devotional insight from both Old and New Testaments came together in a poem he ran in his newspaper column. Like a newsboy standing on the corner of a cold London street shouting, "News! News! Read all about it!" James was shouting in the poetic refrain, "Come and worship, come and worship, worship Christ, the newborn King!"

The music for this carol was written by an Englishman who had lost his sight. Henry Smart was a highly respected organist in the British Isles. Not only did he play the organ and write this great Advent tune, but Smart also designed and built some of the finest organs in England and Scotland. He also composed many exceptional melodies such as the majestic one used with the text for "Lead on, O King Eternal."

Although he was without eyesight the last fifteen years of his life, Smart continued to poetically visualize the brilliance of the newborn Savior *and* coming King.

The Hymns
WORDS AND MUSIC

O Come, All Ye Faithful

1. O come, all ye faith-ful, joy-ful and tri-um-phant,
2. God of God, Light of Light;
3. Sing, choirs of an-gels, sing in ex-ul-ta-tion,
4. Yea, Lord, we greet thee, born this hap-py morn-ing:

O come ye, O come ye to Beth-le-hem; come and be-hold him
lo, he ab-hors not the Vir-gin's womb: ver-y God, be-
sing, all ye cit-i-zens of heav'n a-bove; glo-ry to God
Je-sus, to thee be all glo-ry giv'n; Word of the Fa-ther,

REFRAIN

born the King of an-gels;
got-ten, not cre-a-ted;
in the high-est; O come, let us a-dore him, O come, let
late in flesh ap-pear-ing;

us a-dore him, O come, let us a-dore him, Christ the Lord.

Latin hymn
Attr. to John Francis Wade, 1751
Tr. by Frederick Oakeley, 1841; alt.

ADESTE FIDELES 6.6.10.5.6.ref.
John Francis Wade's *Cantus Diversi*, 1751

Once in Royal David's City

1. Once in roy-al Da-vid's cit-y stood a low-ly cat-tle shed,
2. He came down to earth from heav-en who is God and Lord of all,
3. And through all his won-drous child-hood he would hon-or and o-bey,
4. And our eyes at last shall see him, through his own re-deem-ing love;
5. Not in that poor low-ly sta-ble, with the ox-en stand-ing by,

where a moth-er laid her ba-by in a man-ger for his bed:
and his shel-ter was a sta-ble, and his cra-dle was a stall:
• love and watch the low-ly maid-en in whose gen-tle arms he lay:
for that child so dear and gen-tle is our Lord in heav'n a-bove,
we shall see him, but in heav-en, set at God's right hand on high;

Mar-y was that moth-er mild, Je-sus Christ her lit-tle child.
with the poor, and mean, and low-ly, lived on earth our Sav-ior ho-ly.
• Chris-tian chil-dren all must be mild, o-be-dient, good as he.
and he leads his chil-dren on to the place where he is gone.
when like stars his chil-dren crowned all in white shall wait a-round.

Cecil Frances Alexander, 1848

IRBY 8.7.8.7.7.7.
Henry J. Gauntlett, 1849

Angels We Have Heard on High

1. An - gels we have heard on high, sweet - ly sing - ing o'er the plains,
2. Shep- herds, why this ju - bi - lee? Why your joy - ous strains pro- long?
3. Come to Beth - le - hem and see him whose birth the an - gels sing;

and the moun- tains in re- ply ech - o back their joy - ous strains.
Say what may the tid- ings be, which in - spire your heav'n- ly song?
come, a - dore on bend- ed knee Christ the Lord, the new - born King.

REFRAIN

Glo - - - - ri - a in ex - cel - sis De - o,

glo - - - - ri - a in ex - cel - sis De - o.

Traditional French carol

GLORIA 7.7.7.7.ref.
Traditional French melody
Arr. by Edward S. Barnes, 1937

Come, Thou Long-Expected Jesus

1. Come, thou long - ex - pect - ed Je - sus, born to set thy peo - ple free;
2. Born thy peo - ple to de - liv - er, born a child and yet a king,

from our fears and sins re - lease us; let us find our rest in thee.
born to reign in us for - ev - er, now thy gra - cious king - dom bring.

Is - rael's strength and con - so - la - tion, hope of all the earth thou art,
By thine own e - ter - nal Spir - it rule in all our hearts a - lone;

dear De - sire of ev - 'ry na - tion, joy of ev - 'ry long - ing heart.
by thine all - suf - fi - cient mer - it, raise us to thy glo - rious throne.

St. 1, 4, Charles Wesley, 1744

HYFRYDOL 8.7.8.7.D.
Rowland Hugh Pritchard, 1855

What Child Is This

1. What child is this, who, laid to rest, on Mar-y's lap is sleep-ing?
2. Why lies he in such mean es-tate, where ox and ass are feed-ing?
3. So bring him in-cense, gold, and myrrh; come, peas-ant, king, to own him;

Whom an-gels greet with an-thems sweet, while shep-herds watch are keep-ing?
Good Chris-tian, fear; for sin-ners here the si-lent Word is plead-ing.
the King of kings sal-va-tion brings, let lov-ing hearts en-throne him.

This, this is Christ the King, whom shep-herds guard and an-gels sing:
Nails, spear, shall pierce him through; the cross be borne for me, for you:
Raise, raise the song on high, the vir-gin sings her lul-la-by:

haste, haste to bring him laud, the babe, the son of Mar-y.
hail, hail the Word made flesh, the babe, the son of Mar-y.
joy, joy for Christ is born, the babe, the son of Mar-y.

Traditional English carol
Adapted by William C. Dix, ca. 1865

GREENSLEEVES 8.7.8.7.ref.
English melody, 16th cent.

O Come, O Come, Emmanuel

1. O come, O come, Em - man - u - el, and ran - som cap - tive
2. O come, O come, thou Lord of might, who to thy tribes, on
3. O come, thou Rod of Jes - se, free thine own from Sa - tan's
4. O come, thou Day- spring from on high, and cheer us by thy
5. O come, thou Key of Da - vid, come and o - pen wide our

Is - ra - el, that mourns in lone - ly ex - ile here,
Si - nai's height, in an - cient times didst give the law
• tyr - an - ny; from depths of hell thy peo - ple save,
draw - ing nigh; dis - perse the gloom - y clouds of night,
heav'n - ly home; make safe the way that leads on high,

REFRAIN

un - til the Son of God ap - pear.
in cloud and maj - es - ty and awe.
• and give them vic - t'ry o'er the grave. Re - joice! Re - joice! Em -
and death's dark shad - ows put to flight.
and close the path to mis - er - y.

man - u - el shall come to thee, O Is - ra - el.

Latin antiphons, 12th cent.
Latin hymn, 1710
Tr. by John Mason Neale, 1851; alt. 1961

VENI EMMANUEL L.M.ref.
Plainsong, 13th cent.
Arr. by Thomas Helmore, 1856

O Little Town of Bethlehem

1. O little town of Bethlehem, how still we see thee lie;
2. For Christ is born of Mary; and gathered all above,
3. How silently, how silently, the wondrous gift is giv'n!
4. O holy child of Bethlehem, descend to us, we pray;

above thy deep and dreamless sleep the silent stars go by:
while mortals sleep, the angels keep their watch of wond'ring love.
So God imparts to human hearts the blessings of his heav'n.
cast out our sin and enter in; be born in us today.

yet in thy dark streets shineth the everlasting Light;
O morning stars, together proclaim the holy birth!
No ear may hear his coming, but in this world of sin,
We hear the Christmas angels the great glad tidings tell;

the hopes and fears of all the years are met in thee tonight.
And praises sing to God the King, and peace to men on earth.
where meek souls will receive him still, the dear Christ enters in.
O come to us, abide with us, our Lord Emmanuel.

Phillips Brooks, 1868

ST. LOUIS C.M.D.irreg.
Lewis H. Redner, 1868

Let All Mortal Flesh Keep Silence

Unison

1. Let all mor - tal flesh keep si - lence, and with fear and
2. King of kings, yet born of Mar - y, as of old on
3. Rank on rank the host of heav - en spreads its van - guard
4. At his feet the six - winged ser - aph; cher - u - bim, with

trem - bling stand; pon - der noth - ing earth - ly - mind - ed,
earth he stood, Lord of lords, in hu - man ves - ture,
on the way, as the Light of light de - scend - eth
sleep - less eye, veil their fac - es to the pres - ence,

for with bless - ing in his hand, Christ our God to
in the bod - y and the blood, he will give to
from the realms of end - less day, that the pow'rs of
as with cease - less voice they cry, "Al - le - lu - ia,

earth de - scend - eth, our full hom - age to de - mand.
all the faith - ful his own self for heav'n - ly food.
hell may van - ish as the dark - ness clears a - way.
al - le - lu - ia, al - le - lu - ia, Lord Most High!"

Liturgy of St. James, 5th cent.
Adapted by Gerard Moultrie, 1864

PICARDY 8.7.8.7.8.7.
French melody, 17th cent.
Arr. by Ralph Vaughan Williams, 1906

— 123 —

Silent Night! Holy Night!

1. Si - lent night! Ho - ly night! All is calm, all is bright round yon virgin moth - er and child. Ho - ly in - fant, so ten - der and mild, sleep in heav - en - ly peace, sleep in heav - en - ly peace.

2. Si - lent night! Ho - ly night! Shep - herds quake at the sight! Glo - ries stream from heav - en a - far, heav'n - ly hosts sing al - le - lu - ia; Christ, the Sav - ior, is born! Christ, the Sav - ior, is born!

3. Si - lent night! Ho - ly night! Son of God, love's pure light ra - diant beams from thy ho - ly face, with the dawn of re - deem - ing grace, Je - sus, Lord, at thy birth, Je - sus, Lord, at thy birth.

4. Si - lent night! Ho - ly night! Won - drous star, lend thy light; with the an - gels let us sing al - le - lu - ia to our King; Christ, the Sav - ior, is born! Christ, the Sav - ior, is born!

Joseph Mohr, 1818
Tr. ca. 1850

STILLE NACHT Irreg.
Franz Gruber, 1818

Hark! the Herald Angels Sing

1. Hark! the her - ald an - gels sing, "Glo - ry to the new-born King;
2. Christ, by high - est heav'n a - dored, Christ, the ev - er - last - ing Lord!
3. Hail the heav'n - born Prince of Peace! Hail the Sun of Right - eous- ness!

peace on earth, and mer - cy mild, God and sin - ners rec - on - ciled!"
Late in time be - hold him come, off - spring of the Vir - gin's womb.
Light and life to all he brings, ris'n with heal - ing in his wings.

Joy - ful, all ye na - tions, rise, join the tri - umph of the skies;
Veiled in flesh the God-head see; hail th'in - car - nate De - i - ty,
Mild he lays his glo - ry by, born that man no more may die,

with th'an - gel - ic host pro - claim, "Christ is born in Beth - le - hem!"
pleased as man with men to dwell, Je - sus, our Em - man - u - el.
born to raise the sons of earth, born to give them sec - ond birth.

REFRAIN

Hark! the her - ald an - gels sing, "Glo - ry to the new- born King."

Charles Wesley, 1739, 1753; alt.

MENDELSSOHN 7.7.7.7.D. ref.
Felix Mendelssohn-Bartholdy, 1840
Arr. by William H. Cummings. 1856

— 125 —

Lo, How a Rose E'er Blooming

1. Lo, how a rose e'er bloom-ing from ten-der
2. I - sa - iah 'twas fore - told it, the rose I
3. The shep - herds heard the sto - ry, pro - claimed by
4. This flow'r, whose fra - grance ten - der with sweet - ness
5. O Sav - ior, child of Mar - y, who felt our

stem hath sprung, of Jes - se's lin - eage com - ing,
have in mind; with Mar - y we be - hold it,
• an - gels bright, how Christ, the Lord of glo - ry,
fills the air, dis - pels with glo - rious splen - dor
hu - man woe; O Sav - ior, King of glo - ry,

as men of old have sung. It came, a flow'r - et bright,
the vir - gin moth - er kind. To show God's love a - right
• was born on earth this night. To Beth - le - hem they sped
the dark - ness ev - 'ry - where. True man, yet ver - y God;
who dost our weak - ness know, bring us at length, we pray,

a - mid the cold of win - ter, when half-spent was the night.
she bore to men a Sav - ior, when half-spent was the night.
• and in the man - ger found him, as an - gel her - alds said.
from sin and death he saves us and light-ens ev - 'ry load.
to the bright courts of heav - en and to the end - less day

German hymn, ca. 1500
St. 1-2 tr. by Theodore Baker, 1894
St. 3-4 tr. by Harriett R. Spaeth, 1875
St. 5 tr. by John C. Mattes, 1914

ES IST EIN' ROS' ENTSPRUNGEN 7.6.7.6.6.7.6.
German melody, 15th cent.
Arr. by Michael Praetorius, 1609; alt.

Angels, from the Realms of Glory

1. An - gels, from the realms of glo - ry, wing your flight o'er all the earth;
2. Shep - herds in the fields a - bid - ing, watch- ing o'er your flocks by night,
3. Sa - ges, leave your con - tem- pla- tions, bright- er vi - sions beam a - far;
4. Saints be - fore the al - tar bend-ing, watch- ing long in hope and fear,
5. All cre - a - tion, join in prais- ing God the Fa - ther, Spir - it, Son;

ye who sang cre - a - tion's sto - ry, now pro - claim Mes - si - ah's birth:
God with man is now re - sid - ing, yon- der shines the in - fant Light:
seek the great De - sire of na - tions; ye have seen his na - tal star:
sud - den - ly the Lord, de - scend- ing, in his tem - ple shall ap- pear:
ev - er- more your voic- es rais- ing to th'e - ter - nal Three in One:

REFRAIN

Come and wor- ship, come and wor- ship, wor- ship Christ, the new- born King.

James Montgomery, 1816, 1825

REGENT SQUARE 8.7.8.7.8.7.
Henry Smart, 1867